DISCIPLINES
OF THE
Heart

Cultivating True Devotion for God

KATHLEEN HENDERSON

Acknowledgements

My special thanks to my father, Warren Henderson, for his extensive review of this book and his scriptural insights. Thank you also for your help with the layout and for walking me through the publication process. I am grateful to Caroline Webb for editing and to Daniel Macy for proofreading; both of your talents and investments added much value to this work.

Disciplines of the Heart – Cultivating True Devotion for God
By Kathleen Henderson
Copyright © 2016

Cover Design: Benjamin Bredeweg

Published by Warren A. Henderson
3769 Indiana Road
Pomona, KS 66076

Perfect Bound ISBN: 978-1-939770-34-9
eBook ISBN: 978-1-939770-35-6

Available in many online retail stores

Endorsement

Kathleen has edited over a dozen of my own books, so it has been a joy to review her own contemplations on the importance of guarding and maintaining proper discipline in one's heart. *Disciplines of the Heart* is divided into three main parts: *The Issues of Life - The Heart of the Matter, Your Heart - The Anatomy of a Spiritual Heart,* and *With All Diligence - Disciplines of the Heart.* These instructive portions are followed by a twenty-lesson study guide to involve the reader in the practical applications conveyed within the text. Kathleen invokes an engaging and personable style to prompt the reader to probe beyond the fanciful veneer of superficial religiosity and honestly examine attitudes which hinder true spirituality. The author rightly applies Scripture to address various topics and issues, while at the same time drawing insights and wisdom from many Bible expositors. The author's goal for this study is clearly stated: "To cultivate hearts that are in accordance with the heart of God, and to please and glorify Him as we grow closer to Him each day." To that end, this father wholeheartedly commends this book to those who desire liberation from heart disorders that suppress godliness and devotion to Christ.

— Warren A. Henderson

Contents

Introduction 1

**PART ONE: THE ISSUES OF LIFE – THE HEART
    OF THE MATTER** **3**

Chapter 1: Does God Have Your Heart? 5
Chapter 2: Falling in Love With the Lord 11
Chapter 3: What Is the Heart? 17
Chapter 4: A Heart After God's Own Heart 21

**PART TWO: YOUR HEART – THE ANATOMY
    OF A SPIRITUAL HEART** **27**

Chapter 5: The Penitent Heart 29
Chapter 6: The Pure Heart 33
Chapter 7: The Perfect Heart 37
Chapter 8: The Prepared Heart 41
Chapter 9: The Purposed Heart 45
Chapter 10: The Protected Heart 49

**PART THREE: WITH ALL DILIGENCE –
    DISCIPLINES OF THE HEART** **55**

Chapter 11: Personal Discipline 57
Chapter 12: The Discipline of Self-Control 63
Chapter 13: The Discipline of Contentment 75
Chapter 14: The Discipline of Thankfulness 83
Chapter 15: The Discipline of Faithfulness 89
Chapter 16: The Discipline of Joy 97
Chapter 17: The Discipline of Patience 103
Chapter 18: The Discipline of Submission 109
Chapter 19: The Discipline of Prayer 115
Chapter 20: The Discipline of Purity 123
Conclusion 137
Endnotes 141

DISCIPLINES OF THE HEART: STUDY GUIDE **151**

Introduction

I enjoy good books. Whenever I attend a Bible conference or visit a Christian bookstore, I usually come away with something and my "to-read" list never seems to get any shorter! There are wonderful biographies out there, helpful commentaries, Christ-centered devotionals, and (especially from authors of by-gone days) challenging calls to sanctification and surrender. However, as I peruse what is offered to young Christian women specifically, I find it is often meager food for the soul: ninety-second-a-day devotionals; "how-to" books that claim to fix life's problems, choices, and confusions; or something called "Christian" fiction. What seems to be lacking is a study of the heart. No, I'm not talking about romance and relationships – there are plenty of those sorts of books to be found! By studying the heart, I mean to examine, not just whether what we *do* pleases God, but rather if what we *are* pleases the Lord. This diagnostic is not about a superficial show of godliness, but about having a heart that delights the Lord. A heart of this caliber will manifest itself in all areas of a person's life, even when no one is watching us.

In Proverbs 4:23, the Lord commands us, *"Keep your heart with all diligence, for out of it spring the issues of life."* Here we learn that what is in our hearts will come out in daily living and that our hearts must be guarded if we want them to beat for God. This book is titled "Disciplines of the Heart," for in it we will examine what the heart is, whose it is, and how we are to exercise discipline over it. In the first part, *The Issues of Life - The Heart of the Matter*, we will begin by asking such questions as: Who has my heart? Am I in love with the Lord Jesus? What exactly is the heart? Do I have a heart like God's heart? In the second part, *Your Heart – The Anatomy of a Spiritual Heart*, we will look at the penitent heart, the pure heart, the perfect heart, the prepared heart, the purposed heart, and the protected heart. In the third part, *With All Diligence – Disciplines of the Heart*, we will

1

examine various heart exercises: self-control, contentment, thankfulness, faithfulness, joy, patience, submission, prayer, and purity.

Over the past few years the Lord has used His Word; Christian books, speakers, and friends; and the convicting influence of the Holy Spirit to teach (and re-teach!) me about devotedness and discipleship. This study is a collection of those thoughts. I could not pretend to have attained to the material here; in fact, this book is chiefly written to myself. The goal of this study is to cultivate hearts that are in accordance with the heart of God, and to please and glorify Him as we grow closer to Him each day.

Part One

The Issues of Life –
The Heart of the Matter

Chapter 1: Does God Have Your Heart?

For you were bought at a price; therefore glorify
God in your body and in your spirit, which are God's.
(1 Cor. 6:20)

Any discussion regarding the heart must begin with the topic of ownership: right now, who or what has your heart? Hearts can be given over to a possession, a person, or a pursuit. But truly, your heart by every right belongs to God. There are at least three good reasons for this. Firstly, He is your sovereign God, and as such He has dominion over all things (Rom. 11:36; Acts 17:28). Secondly, He is your mighty Creator (Col. 1:16; Ps. 24:1-2). If you were to paint a picture, write a song, or build a house, these things would be yours by virtue of the fact that they had originated with you. Similarly, God fashioned the universe out of nothing. We owe our very existence, all we have and are, to Him. Thirdly, if you have accepted Him as your personal Savior, He is your precious Redeemer (1 Pet. 1:19). Not only did God make us, but He bought us back to Himself with His own blood after we had rejected Him and gone our own way. Therefore, as our God, Creator, and Redeemer, He has full rights to ourselves, to our hearts.

A Redeemed Heart

"Redeem" is not a word that is often used nowadays, but this concept must be understood before proceeding further. The word itself means "to buy back,"[1] as if you had purchased something, and then again forked over money to *repurchase* it. Why would you do something like that? Why would anyone?

The most trustworthy book on the planet records the greatest redemption story ever told. There was once a King, the King of Glory. "Glory" is anything and everything that makes a person look good, and this King was truly unique, perfect, majestic. He was so powerful He spoke all the wonders of our world into existence, so loving He created

5

people and placed them in a perfect environment, giving them the opportunity to serve and enjoy Him forever. And for a brief moment in time, everything was perfect.*

Then, the King's subjects turned against Him. In a pathetic attempt to steal the glory that rightfully belonged only to the King, mankind cut themselves off from the only source of life and good. Angels waited with bated breath to see how the King of Glory would react to this outrage. His response would be unthinkable.

The King sent His only Son out from His splendid palace to the squalor of the human realm. There, the Prince of Glory became a member of this very race! Though a few followed Him, He was not honored by mankind. Again, angels watched. Where was retribution? Where was justice?

Justice fell upon the Prince of Glory. He took all the punishment we ever would deserve, and paid the price of our rebellion with His own life. He *bought us back* with His own blood. Jesus Christ, the God-Man, was an able and willing substitute. As a perfect Man He could suffer in the place of a man; as God His sacrifice had infinite value. But all the forces of hell could not keep Him in the grave, and the Prince of Glory rose again and now offers free pardon and abundant life to all who acknowledge their crimes against Him and accept His substitutionary death. He is now highly exalted in heaven.

This is the answer of the God of Glory to the treachery of the human race. We tried to sabotage His glory because we wanted it for ourselves, and He could have done anything He wanted with us. He

---

* Note that the terminology used in this section was chosen to retell the gospel in the style of the parables. However, it is essential to understand what is biblical terminology and what is not, as God has revealed Himself to us through His Word. In Scripture it is the Second Person of the Godhead who is called the *"King of Glory"* and not the Father (Ps. 24). The title of *"King"* is reserved for the Son (Ps. 2:6), although David does use it to speak of God without referencing a specific person of the Trinity (Ps. 5:2, 44:4, 47:2). The term "Prince of Glory" does not appear in Scripture at all; Isaiah does refer to the Son of God as the *"Prince of Peace"* (Isa. 9:6). *"God of Glory"* appears to be a non-specific name of God (Ps. 29:3; Acts 7:2). *"Lord of Glory"* in 1 Corinthians 2:8 is a clear reference to the Lord Jesus; elsewhere the other members of the Trinity are spoken of as the *"Father of Glory"* (Eph. 1:17) and the *"Spirit of Glory"* (1 Pet. 4:14).

chose to redeem us. And in this way – this extraordinary, unimaginable way – He becomes all the more glorious!

There are many, many principles for living a godly life. But the very first thing that needs to happen is the miracle of salvation. Dear reader, if you have never trusted the Lord Jesus Christ as your personal Savior, please do not wait till the last minute; when you slip into eternity it will be too late! Believe that Jesus Christ died for *you*, and that He was buried, and that He rose again the third day (1 Cor. 15:3-4). Receive Him as *your* Lord and Savior, and the Father of Glory will receive you as His own child.

As a redeemed sinner, saved by grace, it is important to note that you cannot "be your own master." These days this is a popular, and no doubt alluring, idea. We are told to chart our own course, to control our own destiny, to be whatever we want to be. We are told this approach to life is expedient, practical, humanistic, or even modern. The fact of the matter is this philosophy simply will not work. I used to hold the idea, subconsciously perhaps, that if I wanted something badly enough and I tried hard enough, it could be obtained. However, the Lord brought situations into my life that I could do nothing about, teaching me that I am a dependent creature, dependent on an all-powerful, all-sustaining God. Sooner or later, everyone must come to a similar conclusion: there are things (many things) which are outside of our control as human beings.

Paul the apostle describes the appropriate reaction of the redeemed: *"For you were bought at a price; therefore glorify God in your body and in your spirit, which are God's"* (1 Cor. 6:20). We are to showcase God's glory to the world in what we do and say, living out His life in front of others so they can see His goodness.

Whose Authority Are You Under?

Moreover, there are only two authority structures in this world: if you are not following God's will, then you are honoring the devil. Satan may let you believe for a while that you are your own master, but you'll be playing into his hand. One day you will find you really do not have control at all; delusional pride and willful sin is enslaving (John 8:34; Rom. 6:16; 2 Pet. 2:19). If you are skeptical of whether or not sin can actually enslave a person, try living a sin-free week! Even though sin may be pleasant for a season, the end of it is rottenness. You will always be controlled by something, but you have this choice: will you be led by sin into more sin, or by the Holy Spirit into deeper fellowship with God?

In Romans 12:1-2, the believer is commanded to yield self to God. Paul later tells Christians that God is active in our lives, enabling us not only to *do* His will, but to *want to do* His will: *"For it is God who works in you both to will and to do for His good pleasure"* (Phil. 2:13). Perhaps you merely "want to want" to serve Him? Be assured that God is working in you, and He will continue to do so until you are both willing and working His good pleasure, for His glory. He is more committed to you being in His will than you are yourself! So, start from where you are today and remember God loves you too much to leave you the way you are.

Do you want the abundant life Christ spoke of in John 10:10? Do you want to experience the supernatural and to enjoy a daily walk with God? May each of us grasp these concepts: who God is, who we are, and what He can do in us through His grace. A handful of disciples *"turned the world upside down"* (Acts 17:6). Consider Christ's words to His disciples in Matthew 16:25: *"For whoever desires to save his life will lose it, but whoever loses his life for My sake will find it."* Living for God is not losing yourself; it is finding and living the life He wants you to have – the one you were intended to live!

How does one cultivate such a lifestyle? It begins in the heart. J. B. Nicholson has said, "We need to be what we need to be before we go and do what needs to be done."[2] A plant needs a good root system before it bears fruit. First, pay attention to your spiritual root system: read the Word, pray, and obey. (We must have an attitude of obedience and submission; God generally does not "waste" revelation on those who refuse to follow what He has already shown them; see John 14:21.) As we see God through His Word, we are changed into His image: *"But we all, with unveiled face, beholding as in a mirror the glory of the Lord, are being transformed into the same image from glory to glory, just as by the Spirit of the Lord"* (2 Cor. 3:18). This will be translated into action: *"the people who know their God shall be strong, and carry out great exploits"* (Dan. 11:32b). Second, consider what fruit is springing from your heart into your life. Spiritual fruit can involve good character, service, and the edification of others. When we think of serving others, we cannot help but think of Christ's example.

He took the form of a bondservant (Phil. 2:7), and at one point even picked up a basin and towel and washed the twenty-four grimy feet of His own fallible disciples, including one who was a traitor (Matt. 20:28). He made the role of the servant glorious; therefore, do all things as joyful service to God Himself (Ps. 100:2; Col. 3:23).

I have been crucified with Christ; it is no longer I who live, but Christ lives in me; and the life which I now live in the flesh I live by faith in the Son of God, who loved me and gave Himself for me (Gal. 2:20).

For to me, to live is Christ, and to die is gain (Phil. 1:21).

...choose for yourselves this day whom you will serve... (Josh. 24:15).

Chapter 2: Falling in Love With the Lord

And you shall love the Lord your God with all your heart,
and with all your soul, and with all your might.
(Deut. 6:5)

Our hearts belong to God. However, in the weakness of our flesh, we find our love for Him is not what it should be. We discover we need to "fall in love" with Him anew. The church at Ephesus, seemingly a model gathering of believers, was soundly rebuked by Christ for leaving their *"first love,"* Himself (Rev. 2:4). Practically speaking, how does a person cultivate a love for God? It has been said, "To know Him is to love Him; to love Him is to serve Him." The answer is simple: the better we know God, the more we will appreciate Him. He is so great, so full of loving-kindness, so excellent in His works, and so wonderful in character – it is very easy to fall in love with someone like this!

Listening to the Lord

Consider for a moment human relationships. When people are "in love," they want to learn more about each other, talk with and about the other person, and spend time together. Indeed, these are the same types of activities that will help us to grow in our understanding and appreciation of Christ. First, it should be our goal to know Him better each day. To do this, we will need to be in His Word, for this is His revelation of Himself to us.

Can you imagine a young woman allowing a letter from her fiancé to lie unopened, gathering dust, on her bedside table? Certainly not! Yet, how often we fail to appreciate the treasure of God's Word. Search the Scriptures as a whole, keeping an open eye and open heart for glimpses of the Savior – He is the central theme of the Bible! It might also be helpful to note various sections of the Word of God that particularly touch your heart and increase your love for the Lord, and to review these periodically. For example, some passages of Scripture that help me renew my love for God are: 2 Samuel 22; Psalms 63, 145; Isaiah 40-43, 53; Ephesians 1:16-23; Philippians 2:5-11; Colossians 1:15-2:15; Hebrews 1:1-14; Revelation 4:11-5:14.

Talking With the Lord

If we love the Lord, another thing we should be doing is talking with Him. Note that communication goes two directions; we must take time to quietly listen, waiting for Him to speak to us as we mediate on His Word. Prayer is the privilege God accords His children; He permits us to come before His throne of grace. In fact, He invites us to boldly approach Him (Heb. 4:15-16). In prayer, we praise and worship God, confess sins, lay hold of God's promises, and present our requests to Him with confidence (see Nehemiah 1:4-11 for a Biblical example of prayer). We are to pray persistently (Luke 11:5-10, 18:1-8), specifically (John 15:7), fervently (Jas. 5:16-18), believingly (Matt. 21:21-22; 1 Tim. 2:8; Jas. 1:5), thankfully (Col. 4:2; Phil. 4:6), and continually (Eph. 6:18; Col. 4:2; 1 Thess. 5:17).[1]

When Scripture instructs us to pray *"without ceasing,"* we understand it does not mean we should be praying every moment of our waking lives; aside from the sheer infeasibility of this, there are other activities to which the Word of God commands us to attend. Matthew Henry comments, "The meaning is not that men should do nothing but pray, but that nothing else we do should hinder prayer in its proper season. Prayer will help forward and not hinder all other lawful business, and every good work."[2] We should not *cease* praying; we should pray on a regular and frequent basis. Communion consists, not of uninterrupted talking, but of a constant presence.

Talking About the Lord

What a person talks about is proof of what is in his or her heart. For various people, this may be sports, politics, personal accomplishments, or even other people. For the Christian, Christ should be a topic that leaps readily from the mind to the tongue. Talk about Him both to other believers and to those who do not believe on Him. As Peter exhorted, *"But sanctify the Lord God in your hearts, and always be ready to give a defense to everyone who asks you a reason for the hope that is in you, with meekness and fear"* (1 Pet. 3:15). Be ready and eager to talk to the lost about the Savior. Scripture also indicates we should speak of Christ

12

to those who are saved: *"Preach the word! Be ready in season and out of season. Convince, rebuke, exhort, with all longsuffering and teaching"* (2 Tim. 4:2). Titus 2:1 echoes the exhortation, saying, *"But as for you, speak the things which are proper for sound doctrine."* The passage then proceeds to list specific instructions for various groups of people (young men, older women, etc.) within the church. The present tense verb for speaking is continuous, meaning that we are to *keep speaking* these things. We all need to be reminded! When you gather with other believers, does the conversation center on idle topics? Or do you seek to uphold Christ, to discuss His Word, to edify others and be edified? This is not to say that you should never discuss any secular topics, but if your heart is full of love for God and excitement over His Word, your conversations will tend to drift seamlessly to spiritual matters.

Spending Time With the Lord

We have already considered that, in deepening our relationship with Christ, we must learn of Him, and talk to and of Him. The final thing we can note from human relationships is that people who love each other look for ways to spend time together. What percentage of your day do you spend at Jesus's feet; that is, spending time with Him and thinking about Him? Certainly this involves reading God's Word and praying, as previously discussed, but this category is broader than these exercises alone. It would be a good challenge to spend some time in personal reflection. Make a list of the things that help you cultivate your relationship with God (e.g. personal quiet times alone, singing, prayer, study, memorizing Scripture, journaling your thoughts), then list what hinders that relationship (e.g. busyness, activities, media, social connections, general distractions). Endeavor to increase the quantity and quality of the items on first list, while making cuts on the time spent on the second list. Leslie Ludy observes, "Sometimes, simply putting healthy boundaries around the 'urgent' things in life can give you the ability to truly have time for what is most important in God's priority list."[3] We will always be surrounded by demands that press upon us and clamor for our attention; however, we ought not to let these distract us from what is truly important.

God not only commands us to reverence Him, but calls us to love Him. Indeed these are related, as Matthew Henry has said, "the warmer our affection to Him the greater will be our veneration for Him; the child that honours his parents no doubt loves them."[4] The Lord deserves our delight and devotion. Love for God is, indeed, the first commandment: *"And you shall love the Lord your God with all your heart, with all your soul, with all your mind, and with all your strength. This is the first commandment"* (Mark 12:30). Matthew Henry explains what it means to love the Lord with all our heart, and soul, and might:

> We are also commanded to love God *with all our heart, and soul, and might;* that is, we must love Him, [1.] With a sincere love; not in word and tongue only, saying we love Him when our hearts are not with Him, but inwardly, and in truth, solacing ourselves in Him. [2.] With a strong love; the heart must be carried out towards Him with great ardour and fervency of affection. Some have hence thought that we should avoid saying (as we commonly express ourselves) that we will do this or that with all our heart, for we must not do anything with all our heart but love God; and that this phrase, being here used concerning that sacred fire, should not be unhallowed. He that is our all must have our all, and none but He. [3.] With a superlative love; we must love God above any creature whatsoever, and love nothing besides Him but what we love for Him and in subordination to Him. [4.] With an intelligent love; for so it is explained, Mar. 12:33. To love Him with all the heart, and with all the understanding, we must know Him, and therefore love Him as those that see good cause to love Him. [5.] With an entire love; He is one, and therefore our hearts must be united in this love, and the whole stream of our affections must run towards Him. O that this love of God may be shed abroad in our hearts![5]

We love Him for the awesomeness of who He is, for the delightfulness of His character, for the benevolence of His works: *"We love Him because He first loved us"* (1 Jn. 4:19). We can love as only He can because we have experienced His love. Heartfelt love for God is His first commandment; it should be our first priority. Love the Lord your God.

What Can You Do With Your Whole Heart?

- Seek God (Deut. 4:29; Josh. 22:5; Ps. 119:2, 10; Jer. 29:13)
- Praise God (Ps. 9:1, 86:12, 111:1, 138:1)
- Observe God's Law; that is, His Word (Ps. 119:34, 69)
- Entreat God (Ps. 119:58)
- Believe God (Acts 8:37)
- Repent to God (Joel 2:12)
- Be glad and rejoice in God (Zeph. 3:14)
- Love God (Deut. 6:5; Matt. 22:37; Mark 12:30, 33; Luke 10:27)

Chapter 3: What Is the Heart?

Now may the God of peace Himself sanctify you completely;
and may your whole spirit, soul, and body be preserved
blameless at the coming of our Lord Jesus Christ.
(1 Thess. 5:23)

We sometimes speak of the heart as a symbol of love or zeal. We also speak of it in the purely anatomical sense as a four-chambered, blood-pumping organ. We can metaphorically say a person has "a heart of stone" or "a heart of a lion," or spiritually, that God has conferred us with "a new heart." And so it is with good reason we pause to ask: what is in view when the word "heart" is used in the Bible? Certainly there are references to the physical organ, but as Warren Henderson explains, "more generally the word speaks of an invisible component of the human soul relating to emotions, desires, moral inclinations, and cognitive abilities. Figuratively, the heart is the hidden spring of the personal and inward life."[1] We see that the heart is not merely a symbol of attraction or ardor, but rather it is an integral part of each person, involving the feelings, will, and intellect.

Spirit, Soul, and Body

Scripture tells us a whole person is comprised of spirit, soul, and body (1 Thess. 5:23). Of these, we understand best the body, as it is something we see. The body is not eternal, as every cemetery testifies. It is physical and is conscious of the earth. On the other hand, the soul is conscious of self. The soul is the entire personality; it is what makes you, you. It is eternal (man cannot destroy it – Matt. 10:28; see also Rev. 6:9). The spirit is also eternal (Eccl. 12:7); it is God-conscious. It includes the moral conscience God has given each of us: His law written within ourselves in order for us to know what is right and what is wrong (Rom. 2:15). Elihu remarked, *"But there is a spirit in man, and the breath of the Almighty gives him understanding"* (Job 32:8).

We read in Proverbs: *"The spirit of a man is the lamp of the Lord, searching all the inner depths of his heart"* (20:27). Thus, the body is animal, the soul is human, and the spirit is heavenly. The spirit and soul are eternal, while the body is temporal. However, believers are promised a new, glorified body (1 Cor. 15:35-58). Throughout eternity the redeemed will worship and serve God with a perfect spirit, soul, and body.

Heart, Mind, and Soul

The soul includes the mind and the heart, as these are each a part of one's personality. In fact, one could say the heart is the core of the soul; Scripture tells us it is responsible for emotions (Prov. 14:10; John 16:22; Rom. 9:2), personal morality (Jer. 17:9; Matt. 15:19), the will (Acts 11:23; 2 Cor. 9:7; Heb. 4:12), and cognition (Mark 2:6; Luke 1:51; Heb. 4:12). In consideration of the last aspect, the heart can be said to envelop the mind. Warren Henderson describes the mind itself as the "seat of reflective consciousness."[2] It is able to perceive, to comprehend, to rationalize, to remember, and to determine. However, it is influenced by the heart.

In his book, *Forsaken, Forgotten, and Forgiven: A Devotional Study of Jeremiah*, Warren Henderson finds a general distinction between the Hebrew words used in Scripture to reference the heart and those used to refer to the mind.[3] A study of the New Testament Greek reveals this language also uses different words to speak of the heart, the mind, and the soul. The Lord's own words in Mark 12:30 confirm a difference between these three. From a general survey of Scripture, it seems it is more correct to speak of the heart when discussing "moral character or issues of personal life";[4] of the mind when speaking of perception, understanding, and reasoning; and of the soul when referencing the individual himself or herself (e.g. Isa. 55:3; Acts 2:43). Accordingly, the writers of the New Testament focused their discussion more on the specific components of the soul (i.e. the heart and mind), rather than on the soul itself.[5]

The Heart of the Matter

In our efforts to understand these things, we try to compartmentalize our own components; we often fall into the same error when we contemplate the Trinity. In neither case can the parts be separated from the whole. Ties and interlinkages abound; the spirit includes the conscience which affects the heart of the soul (Acts 2:37; 1 Jn. 3:20), which, in turn, influences the mind (the heart has cognitive properties) and will (1 Cor. 7:37). Gerald Cowen helps to explain why the Bible does not exclusively distinguish each component; this also clarifies why some overlap in terminology is allowed. He begins with the observation that in our culture,

> … the mind is considered to be the center of the person. However, in Scripture the heart is more often considered to be the center of human personality. In the Old Testament, especially, this is true because of the lack of an exact [Hebrew] equivalent for *mind*. The word *heart* fills this void, and the New Testament follows the practice of the Old Testament very closely. Why then can the mind as well as the heart be spoken of as the center of a person? Because in Hebrew thought a person is looked at as a single entity with no attempt to compartmentalize the person into separate parts which act more or less independently of one another. Therefore, the heart, mind, and soul, while in some ways different, are seen as one.[6]

We as humans are unable to separate spirit, soul, and body, and our personality in its entirety is revealed in our soul, heart, and mind. Clearly, we cannot expect to have a good mind if we have a bad heart. Each part of ourselves is a part of each part as much as it is a part of the whole.

In conclusion, each of us is spirit, soul, and body. The soul encompasses human personality and at its center is the heart, which involves the emotions, personal morality, the will, and cognition. We would do well to end this chapter by making an examination of our own hearts. Is your heart healthy? Jeremiah tells us, *"The heart is deceitful above all things, and desperately wicked; who can know it?"* (Jer. 17:9). This is the natural state of the human heart and is why Solomon said, *"He who trusts in his own heart is a fool"* (Prov. 28:26). It is beyond conservative therapy; we need a spiritual heart transplant! God confers new hearts, and just the heart we need (1 Sam. 10:9; Jer. 32:39; Ezek. 11:19, 36:26). The Lord's answer to the problem posed by Jeremiah is: *"Then I will give them a heart to know Me, that I am the Lord; and they shall be My people, and I will be their God, for they shall return to Me with their whole heart"* (Jer. 24:7). Let us have such a heart!

Thou hast formed us for Thyself, and our hearts are restless until they rest in Thee.

— Augustine[7]

Chapter 4: A Heart After God's Own Heart

...He raised up for them David as king, to whom also He gave
testimony and said, I have found David the son of Jesse,
a man after My own heart, who will do all My will.
(Acts 13:22b)

Scripture says much about David, *"the sweet psalmist of Israel"* (2 Sam. 23:1), and arguably the nation's mightiest king, but perhaps the most significant thing about this man is that God declared he was *"a man after My own heart"* (Acts 13:22; see 1 Sam. 13:14). First Samuel 16 emphasizes just how unnoticed David was as a young man. He was left with the rather unglamorous task of keeping the sheep while everyone else gathered to sacrifice and enjoy a good dinner with the notable prophet Samuel. His own father did not think to call him home when Samuel began to size up his older seven brothers with the idea of identifying Israel's future king. Samuel himself thought one of David's brothers would be God's selection, but that was not the case. But David was the type of man whom God saw, and in His timing God led others to notice and approve of him also. And so the shepherd lad became the anointed king of Israel.

God Examines Hearts

The first thing to learn from this is how God views the human heart: observe what He told Samuel as He redirected his gaze away from the oldest of Jesse's sons:

> *But the Lord said to Samuel, "Do not look at his appearance or at his physical stature, because I have refused him. For the Lord does not see as man sees; for man looks at the outward appearance, but the Lord looks at the heart"* (1 Sam. 16:7).

He knows the secrets of the heart (Ps. 44:21). He discerns the thoughts and intents of the heart (Luke 9:47; Heb. 4:12). In the words of George Herbert, "God sees hearts as we see faces."[1] In light of this, it behooves us to be careful on what we muse, even in the best-concealed recess of the heart. The Bible records many instances where people got into trouble because of what they *said* silently in their hearts (e.g. Deut. 8:17; Isa. 9:9; Zeph. 1:12; Matt. 24:48). Also, recall how Sarah was rebuked for *laughing* within her heart when God promised her a son (Gen. 18:12). Furthermore, Michal was judged because she *despised* David in her heart; as her husband and her king, David was in a position of authority, and she should have respected him (2 Sam. 6:16). Take care what you say, laugh at, or despise in your heart!

The Heart God Approves

The second thing to learn from the anointing of David is that God not only looks at the heart, but He considers its condition highly important. When God set about to choose a king for His people, He did not look for someone who was a good speaker, or who had professional skills, or who was well-known, or who dwelt with the sons of the prophets (2 Kgs. 6:1), or who had been to Bible school – no, God was looking for a man after His own heart: a man who, unlike King Saul, would obey Him, who would do His will. Jehovah's gaze came to rest on the shepherd boy David.

Having a heart like God's is not something that sporadically occurs in random individuals. The key is obedience. God is holy and can have no fellowship with anyone in sin (1 Jn. 1:5-6). He is the eternal, unchanging God. If, then, we desire to have a heart like His, we must be willing to allow God to conform our priorities and our will to be like His.

The same passage of Scripture that refers to David as a man after God's own heart describes him as someone who longed to do all God's will (Acts 13:22). He desired what God desired, and would therefore do what God wanted. David was not perfect, but he had a strong commitment to obedience. As a result, he experienced a close relationship with his God. Our obedience to God determines the degree of fellowship we have with Him. I have often heard my father say, "You are as close to the Lord now as you want to be." As your heart becomes more like God's heart through obedience, you will draw nearer to Him. Obedience proves you love God, and an obedient heart delights God: *"He who has My commandments and keeps them, it is he who loves Me. And he who loves Me will be loved by My Father, and I will love him and manifest Myself to him"* (John 14:21). You may not know much now, but live according to what you do know, obey what you do know (Phil. 3:15-16). Then, God will show you more and more.

Do you desire to do the will of God? Do you want what God wants? I had the privilege of hearing an excellent message on the will of God by Scott DeGroff. He emphasized that to have this kind of heart one must be committed to the revealed will of God (what He has declared in His Word), and trust Him to make known His specific direction in one's personal life. God has disclosed much of His will to us; search out the commands in the Bible and obey them. The Bible is also our guide for understanding what His specific will is for each of us believers; God will never ask you to do something contradictory to His Word. When seeking God's guidance, approach opportunities with prayer (Prov. 16:1, 9; Jas. 1:5). Seek out wise counsel (Prov. 11:14). Look for the inner witness of the Holy Spirit; He constrains and He compels – consider whether you have the peace of God in a matter (Col. 3:15). Lastly, if the desires of your heart are God-honoring, wait patiently on the Lord to either fulfill or refine these (Ps. 37:4).[2]

It is fine to have a will, to have heart-longings, as long as these are not in contradiction with the will of God. Paul clearly had a will, and he did not apologize for this, though he endeavored to keep it in subjection to God's will (Rom. 1:10-11). Whenever you make plans, make sure you have "divine override" authorized!   Be open to His direction in life's interruptions and inconveniences. Do not seek after your own heart (Num. 15:39); follow what is in God's heart and in His mind (1 Sam. 2:35). This is the best way. Jeremiah stated, *"The heart is deceitful above all things, and desperately wicked; who can know it?"* (Jer. 17:9). This verse was mentioned in the last chapter in relation to the unregenerate. However, even after salvation, a person's heart is one of the least reliable things in which to trust. Sometimes even a well-meaning heart will lead you astray (2 Sam. 7:3; Job 15:12). Hence, it is important to seek the heart of God through prayer and the study of His Word.

The Influence of a Healthy Heart

What does a person look like, whose heart beats in time with God's own heart? What characterized David's life? He sang and praised God, he was faithful with what was entrusted to him, he respected the authorities in his life, he was willing to wait for God's timing, he trusted in God's vindication concerning his accusers, and he was courageous in all that he did. His aspirations and priorities are revealed in his psalms:

When You said, "Seek My face," my heart said to You, "Your face, Lord, I will seek" (Ps. 27:8).

A Psalm of David, when he was in the wilderness of Judah: O God, You are my God; early will I seek You: my soul thirsts for You, my flesh longs for You in a dry and thirsty land where there is no water (Ps. 63:1).

May a closer relationship with God be the desire of our hearts also, and may our lives be marked by praise, faithfulness, respect for authority, patience, and courage. It would be wonderful if you could be called "a woman after God's own heart!"

The heart influences what one says (Matt. 12:34-35), and situations arise (brought about by God!) that will reveal what is in one's heart (2 Chron. 32:31). Thus are the secrets of our hearts made manifest (1 Cor. 14:25). A little heart-searching is, therefore, in order. Consider the following questions:

- Is my heart broken and contrite? (Ps. 24:4, 51:17, 139:23-24)
- How close is my heart to God? (Isa. 29:13; Ezek. 33:30-32)
- What is the desire of my heart? (Ps. 37:4)
- Is my heart like the Lord's heart? (Acts 13:22)

Oh God, my heart is not like Your heart. Will You please take my heart out, and put Yours in me? May the words You spoke through the prophet Ezekiel regarding Israel's restoration be true in my life also: *"I will give you a new heart and put a new spirit within you; I will take the heart of stone out of your flesh and give you a heart of flesh"* (Ezek. 36:26, see also 11:19). The Lord lamented the fact that the nation of

Israel drew near to Him with their mouth, but their heart was far from Him (Matt. 15:8; Mark 7:6). Let us not repeat their error. Pour out your heart to the Lord (Ps. 62:8; Lam. 2:19); lift up your heart to Him (Lam. 3:41); incline your heart toward Him (Josh. 24:23; Ps. 119:36, 112, 141:4). Have a heart after God's heart.

Robert Pierce, founder of World Vision and Samaritan's Purse, has the following written on the flyleaf of his Bible: "Let my heart be broken with the things that break the heart of God."[3]

Part Two

Your Heart – The Anatomy
of a Spiritual Heart

Chapter 5: The Penitent Heart

If I regard iniquity in my heart, the Lord will not hear me.
(Ps. 66:18)

In the first portion of this book, we learned the heart is the center of one's personality and involves the emotions, moral character, will, and cognition. We also looked at foundational matters such as God's claim to our heart and our need for a heart like God's heart. In Part Two, *Your Heart - Anatomy of a Spiritual Heart*, we will take a closer look at the heart that pleases God and find Scripture describes it as one that is penitent, pure, perfect, prepared, purposed, and protected.

The first type of heart we will look at is the penitent heart. There is good reason for beginning our study here. Penitence is the first and on-going requirement of a walk with God. It is defined as "feeling or expressing sorrow for sin or wrongdoing and disposed to atonement and amendment; repentant; contrite."[1] This heart is truly sorry, not merely for sin's discovery or consequences, but for the offense of sin itself. It is repentant, turning away from sin and turning to God. Unless we have reached this point, our hearts will never be close to the heart of God.

The Need for a Penitent Heart

God is holy, and He does not change. On the other hand, Paul tells us in no uncertain terms, *"As it is written: 'There is none righteous, no, not one; there is none who understands; there is none who seeks after God. They have all turned aside; they have together become unprofitable; there is none who does good, no, not one'"* (Rom. 3:10-12). Sin separates the sinner from God like a cloud that hides the sun (see Isa. 59:2). As a member of the fallen human race, the heart you were born with is horridly wicked, rotten through and through. You are capable of more loathsome atrocities than you can even imagine. This heart cannot be reformed; it must be spiritually transformed, which

29

means all of its previous intents must be replaced. God offers a heart transplant, so to speak; He will get rid of our old heart, and present us with a new one (Ezek. 11:19).

Accordingly, the first aspect of a penitent heart must lead to salvation. You must acknowledge Jesus as Lord, believing that God raised Him from the dead after He bore the punishment for our sins at Calvary:

> *But what does it say? The word is near you, in your mouth and in your heart (that is, the word of faith which we preach): that if you confess with your mouth the Lord Jesus and believe in your heart that God has raised Him from the dead, you will be saved.* ***For with the heart one believes unto righteousness****, and with the mouth confession is made unto salvation* (Rom. 10:8-10, emphasis added).

Note that this is a heart-knowledge, not merely a head-knowledge. It is not enough to believe in God; you must trust in His solution for sin – Christ (Jas. 2:19). Knowing the truth is not enough to save a person; it is necessary to act on the truth, truly trusting Him from the heart. It is possible to draw near to the Lord with our lips, and yet have a heart that does not know Him (Matt. 7:21-23), or that is very far from Him (Matt. 15:8). As Matthew Henry says, we must seek Him "with a true heart, without any allowed guile or hypocrisy. God is the searcher of hearts, and He requires truth in the inward parts."[2] Have you ever acknowledged yourself a sinner before God, deserving of His judgment, accepting of His salvation?

Penitence is not a one-time attitude that is finished once a person acknowledges he or she is a condemned sinner in need of a Savior. The psalmist wrote, *"If I regard iniquity in my heart, the Lord will not hear me"* (Ps. 66:18, KJV). What a solemn thought! Although nothing can break the relationship between the child of God and the heavenly Father (John 10:28-29), sin severs the Christian's fellowship with God, for He is holy and cannot have sin near Him. We are warned in Psalm 66 that the Lord will not hear our prayers if we discern iniquity in our hearts and do nothing about it.

We must keep short accounts with the Lord. There is a story told about the great preacher C. H. Spurgeon that illustrates this. One day, Spurgeon was out walking with a friend of his:

Spurgeon…suddenly stopped in the middle of the street he was crossing and prayed. When he reached the other side, his companion asked him, "Why did you stop to pray in the middle of the street?" Spurgeon's reply was something like this, "A cloud came between my soul and Christ, and I could not let it remain there even long enough to reach the other side of the street."[3]

Do we have this same sensitivity to sin?

Confessing Sin

It would be worthwhile to briefly address the difference between asking forgiveness for sin and confessing it. For the majority of my life, when confronted with sin I have asked the Lord to forgive me, often repeatedly asking forgiveness for the same occurrence. Also, either from a desire to "cover everything" or "save time," I tend to be vague and general in these prayers (i.e. "please forgive me for my sin"). Recently, however, I have learned that asking forgiveness is not exactly the same thing as confessing sin. When I confess a sin, I go before God and specifically state what I have done wrong, agreeing with Him that it is sin. It is a little harder on one's pride to state "I did such and such, and this is clearly wrong" than to glibly say "please forgive me" (or, worse, "I am willing to be forgiven!"); I think the former better captures the biblical principles of repentance, humility, and confession of sins. Note that we are commanded to *confess* our sins; it is not a Scriptural practice to repeatedly beg forgiveness for a sin once confessed – God promises to forgive confessed sin and to cleanse us (1 Jn. 1:9)!

Is there unconfessed sin in your life? Take the time to carefully and prayerfully examine your heart. It has been said that there are sins of commission and sins of omission. Sins of commission are wrong things we do, and examples are: gossip, slander, impurity, unrighteous anger, hatred, and disobedience of authorities. Sins of omission are the right things we do not do, and these could include: lack of love for God and His people, lack of concern for lost souls, wasting time and other resources, failing to speak for God, and a lack of discipline. Additionally, Psalm 90:8 speaks of *"secret sins"*; these could be things like bitterness, envy, and unthankfulness that we hide from others (and maybe even ourselves) but cannot hide from God. Another psalm refers to *"presumptuous sins"* (19:13), which are pride in all its many forms: preoccupation with self, boasting, insistence on doing things your way, lack of submission to God, and so forth. May we be contrite, humbly agreeing with God on the matter of sin, and confess and turn away from it. We have this promise: *"If we confess our sins, He is faithful and just to forgive us our sins and to cleanse us from all unrighteousness"* (1 Jn. 1:9). May we have penitent hearts.

[Sin] is the dare of God's justice, the rape of His mercy, the jeer of His patience, the slight of His power, and the contempt of His love.

— John Bunyan[4]

Chapter 6: The Pure Heart

Blessed are the pure in heart: for they shall see God.
(Matt. 5:8)

The Greek word for pure is *katharos*, meaning clean, and it can be used in a variety of contexts. First, it can be used in a Levitical sense, signifying ceremonial cleanliness in relation to the Law. Second, it is used in a physical sense to speak both of a vine's pruning process and a fire's refining influence. These two illustrations show us how *katharos* is accomplished. To purify precious metals such as gold or silver, the ancients used a process called cupellation: a powderized mix of metal and rock was placed in a clay crucible, and then heated in a furnace until the dross separated from the desired metal.[1] In much the same way, God brings difficult problems, circumstances, or even people into our lives to refine our character.

The other image invoked by the word *katharos* is pruning. In John 15:2, the Lord says, *"Every branch in Me that does not bear fruit He [lifts it up]*[2] *and every branch that bears fruit He prunes, that it may bear more fruit."* The Master works in our lives to lift us up out of the dirt, carefully pruning us so that our fruitfulness is increased. When we think of metal heated over a fire, or a vine cut down to its stalk, we realize neither process is a particularly comfortable one; however, both produce something precious and useful! So too is God's purification of His children.

Ethical Purity

The third way the word *katharos* can be used is in relation to ethical purity. This refers to genuine blamelessness, freedom "from corrupt desire, from sin and guilt," as Thayer explains.[3] Let us examine each of these areas.

Purity is freedom from corrupt desire. Paul describes how we, before conversion, were led by the cravings of the flesh: *"among whom also we all once conducted ourselves in the lusts of our flesh, fulfilling the desires of the flesh and of the mind, and were by nature children of wrath, just as the others"* (Eph. 2:3). As redeemed children of God, we ought not to be excited by the things of the flesh. Some will make the excuse that it is permissible to toy with the idea of sin as long as one does not actually do it. Lest we be tempted to fall into this line of thought, let us remember we serve the God who equates hatred with murder, and lust with adultery, and covetousness with idolatry (Matt. 5:21-22; Matt. 5:28; Eph. 5:5). This is the God who says, *"The devising of foolishness is sin"* (Prov. 24:9a). Romans 1:32 condemns not only those who do sin, but also those who have pleasure in watching others sin. We are to be led by the Spirit, not by the flesh (Gal. 5:16-17). Moreover, what you allow your mind to dwell on *will* affect you; it is inevitable. Do not, therefore, *allow* your mind to dwell on sinful things.

Purity is freedom from sin. It is not bondage in the same way that tracks do not repress a train; they liberate it to move within boundaries and permit it to be profitable. Purity is holiness in all areas of life. Purity is a direction rather than a demarcation. There are people who imagine that there is some sort of spiritual division with sin on one side and holiness on the other. They try to get as close to sin as possible without actually crossing the line. The pure neither creep nor slide toward impurity; they regard sin as a disgrace, and, keeping their back to it, press on to know the Lord. The question is not, "How much can I do without going too far (or getting caught)?" but rather, "What will please my Lord and Savior, and bring Him honor?" This quality of purity is homogenous holiness, not mixed with anything that defiles. How much dirt does it take before a garment is no longer spotlessly clean? There is no acceptable level of sin in a believer's life; we are to abhor even the stain of the flesh (Jude 23).

Purity is freedom from guilt; it promotes a clear conscience. The writer of Hebrews exhorts, *"Let us draw near with a true heart in full assurance of faith,* **having our hearts sprinkled from an evil conscience,** *and our bodies washed with pure water"* (Heb. 10:22, emphasis added). The blood of Jesus Christ is the only cleansing agent for the stain of sin. Matthew Henry comments:

> Having our hearts sprinkled from an evil conscience, by a believing application of the blood of Christ to our souls. They may be cleansed from guilt, from filth, from sinful fear and torment, from all aversion

to God and duty, from ignorance, and error, and superstition, and whatever evils the consciences of men are subject to by reason of sin.[4]

If we, as Christians, have repented of a sin, we can know that it is cleansed by the blood of Christ. Through the New Covenant sealed by Christ's blood, God has judicially dealt with our sin and therefore can righteously choose not to remember it (Heb. 8:12). We should follow His example. Paul, who had certainly done many regrettable and even horrible things, said, *"forgetting those things which are behind, and reaching forth unto those things which are before, I press toward the mark for the prize of the high calling of God in Christ Jesus"* (Phil. 3:13b-14). It is an error to be enslaved to the memory of sin when God has freed us from its hold!

At this point, we might wonder with Solomon, *"Who can say, 'I have made my heart clean, I am pure from my sin?'"* (Prov. 20:9). First, let us consider the words of Duncan Campbell, a preacher during the revival of 1949-1952 in the Scottish Hebrides: "This desire for heart purity is a creation of the Holy Spirit at work in the heart."[5] We would have neither hope of nor desire for purity if God was not active in our lives. But take heart – He is engaged in such work!

Keeping a Pure Heart

Therefore, let us explore what we can do in this process by looking at some practical ways to keep a pure heart. It is important to saturate our lives with Scripture: God's Word is pure, so feed on it, meditate on it, and conform your life to it (Ps. 119:11,140). Speaking of the Bible, D. L. Moody said, "This Book will keep you from sin, or sin will keep you from this Book."[6] We must beseech the Lord's help in prayer; we can echo David's plea, *"Create in me a clean heart, O God, and renew a steadfast spirit within me"* (Ps. 51:10). If we spend time on our knees before the throne of grace, if we are constantly enjoying the presence of God, then our desire for lesser things will fade. We also need to exercise discipline over our minds. Physically, you are what you eat; spiritually, you are what you think (Prov. 23:7). Therefore, think on what is pure (Phil. 4:8). Commit to the "garbage in, garbage out" rule; if a bad thought comes into your mind, get rid of it and replace it with a good thought! To muse on filth is a violation of your purity!

35

James exhorts us to actively purify our hearts: *"Draw near to God and He will draw near to you. Cleanse your hands, you sinners; and purify your hearts, you double-minded"* (Jas. 4:8). God sees the very cockles of your heart. He knows when we are motivated by pride or hypocrisy. He knows our secret sins. He knows when our heart is not wholly with Him. Purify your heart by ridding it of deceit, distractions, disobediences, and untrue doctrines. Paul likewise exhorts us to call on the Lord out of a pure heart; to do this, it is necessary to flee youthful lusts and instead follow after righteousness, faith, charity, and peace (2 Tim. 2:22). Have a heart that turns away from sin and turns to God.

In closing, note the Bible promises that those who are pure in heart will be blessed. The most prominent of these blessings is close fellowship with God (Ps. 24:3-6; Matt. 5:8). What the psalmist Asaph said long ago is still accurate today: *"Truly God is good to Israel, to such as are pure in heart"* (Ps. 73:1). God is good and does good to the pure in heart.

I would sooner be holy than happy if the two things could be divorced. Were it possible for a man always to sorrow and yet to be pure, I would choose the sorrow if I might win the purity, for to be free from the power of sin, to be made to love holiness, is true happiness.

— Charles Spurgeon[7]

Chapter 7: The Perfect Heart

*And thou, Solomon my son, know thou the God of thy father, and
serve Him with a perfect heart and with a willing mind: for the
Lord searcheth all hearts, and understandeth all the imaginations
of the thoughts: if thou seek Him, He will be found of thee; but if
thou forsake Him, He will cast thee off forever.*
(1 Chron. 28:9, KJV)

What does it mean to have a "perfect" heart? The Hebrew word
rendered "perfect" in 1 Chronicles 28:9 (and in twelve of the thirteen
other times this phrase is found in the Bible) is *shâlêm.*[*] It doesn't
necessarily denote sinless perfection, but rather signifies "completeness
and readiness."[1] Think of some gizmo you might buy that comes with
the ominous label: "Assembly required." It is not fit for anything until
it is fully put together. Similarly, a heart is not designed to be left
fragmented. But the gadget in our illustration was not fabricated just to
sit in its completeness on a shelf gathering dust; no, it was purchased
and assembled for a purpose, to do something! Similarly, if your heart
is *complete*, it will be *ready* for the work that is intended. God has
expectations for your life (Eph. 2:10)!

In the Old Testament, those who had perfect hearts are described as
united, free from false motives, willing, and faithful (1 Chron. 12:38,
28:9, 29:9; 2 Chron. 19:9, KJV). Their hearts were whole, ready for
action, and they were proactive in serving God. The term *"perfect*

---

[*] This Hebrew word is typically translated as "perfect" in the KJV, ASV, and Darby
Translation (and sometimes so in the NKJV); however, the word has a variety of
renditions in other versions, for example:
  2 Chron. 16:9 - "completely His" (NASB, NKJV), "fully committed to Him" (NIV)
  2 Chron. 28:9 - "whole heart" (NASB), "wholehearted devotion" (NIV), "loyal
     heart" (NKJV)
  Ps. 101:2 - "integrity of my heart" (NASB), "blameless heart" (NIV)

heart" is not found in the New Testament; however, the related phrase *"singleness of heart"* is used to speak of sincere service to the Lord; this heart is not self-seeking, stingy, or hypocritical (Eph. 6:5; Col. 3:22).

To summarize, a perfect heart is one that is complete, full, united, and sincere. It has one desire, one love, one attraction. It is devoted and reverent before God. A perfect heart is manifested in faithfulness, willing service, and uprightness. Its motives are pure, its affection undivided. David cried, *"Unite my heart to fear Your name"* (Ps. 86:11b); may this be our aspiration and our prayer.

A Perfect Epitaph

The importance of a perfect heart is reflected in the memorials of the kings of Judah. David (1 Kgs. 11:4, 15:3), Asa (1 Kgs. 15:14; 2 Chron. 15:17), and Hezekiah (2 Kgs. 20:3; Isa. 38:3) are each said to have walked before the Lord with a heart that was *"perfect"* ("whole," ESV; "loyal," NKJV); on the other hand, Scripture records that Solomon (1 Kgs. 11:4) and Abijam (1 Kgs. 15:3) did not. Think of all the things that could have been said about these men: construction projects, palace refurbishments, political gains, battles, and conquests – what is it that Scripture records about them? When all is said and done, each man's life boiled down to this one thing: did he walk before the Lord with a perfect heart? Of all epitaphs, we could wish for none greater than: This woman did what was right in the eyes of the Lord with a perfect heart all the days of her life.

As his own life drew to a close, a perfect heart is what King David prayed for his son Solomon: *"And give unto Solomon my son a perfect heart, to keep Thy commandments, Thy testimonies, and Thy statutes, and to do all these things, and to build the* [temple], *for the which I have made provision"* (1 Chron. 29:19, KJV). This is certainly a good prayer for one's children, family, friends, and oneself. Let us keep God's Word and do His work with a perfect heart.

Sadly, we read King Solomon *"... did that which was right in the sight of the Lord, but not with a perfect heart"* (2 Chron. 25:2, KJV). He had a godly heritage, but lacked personal commitment to God. We cannot live under the spiritual shadow of a godly man or woman; if we lack a personal walk with the Lord, our faith will not stand. Abraham's nephew Lot made this discovery. Abraham was *faithful*, but Lot was a *follower* and consequently suffered much from his carnal choices (Gen. 19). Like Lot, such people may in fact be saved, but they will not experience the heavenly life while on earth, and they will certainly have nothing to show for eternity (2 Pet. 2:7-8).

The Necessity of a Perfect Heart

Another thing we learn from Solomon is that it is possible to do right things, and yet these have no value if the works accomplished do not arise from a heart that is perfect before God. In such a way believers lose eternal rewards. Even more sobering, Christ Himself warned that on judgment day some will claim to have done good works in His name; however, they have never been regenerated and thus all their actions arise from an impure heart:

> *Many will say to Me in that day, "Lord, Lord, have we not prophesied in Your name, cast out demons in Your name, and done many wonders in Your name?" And then I will declare to them, "I never knew you; depart from Me, you who practice lawlessness!"* (Matt. 7:22-23).

These are chilling words: it is possible to know things about the Lord and do things in His name and still not be His! There will be many people, many religious people, many "good" people, to whom the Lord will say, "I never knew you; depart from Me!" Dear reader, make sure that you have received Christ as Savior and then, through the power of God's indwelling Spirit, pursue a perfect heart – don't let anything turn you aside from this aspiration. King Solomon started out as a godly young man. Eventually, his many wives introduced idolatry into his life – relationships led Solomon's heart away from the Lord (1 Kgs. 11:4). If anything or any person supplants Christ's rightful place as your first love, then that is sin!

In closing, examine the charge, the resolution, and the promise of a perfect heart. Understanding that it is our reasonable service to serve God faithfully from the heart, each individual ought to make a personal resolution to walk before the Lord with a perfect heart. And for those who do have hearts completely, sincerely devoted to God, they can be encouraged in that God promises to show Himself strong on their behalf.

The Charge:
*"Let your heart therefore be **perfect** with the LORD our God, to walk in His statutes, and to keep His commandments, as at this day"* (1 Kgs. 8:61, KJV). *"And he charged them, saying, 'Thus shall ye do in the fear of the LORD, faithfully, and with a **perfect** heart'"* (2 Chron. 19:9, KJV).

The Resolution:
*"I will behave wisely in a **perfect** way. Oh, when will You come to me? I will walk within my house with a **perfect** heart"* (Ps. 101:2). *"Teach me Your way, O LORD; I will walk in Your truth; **unite** my heart to fear Your name"* (Ps. 86:11).

The Promise:
*"For the eyes of the LORD run to and fro throughout the whole earth, to [show] Himself strong in the behalf of them whose heart is **perfect** toward Him..."* (2 Chron. 16:9a, KJV).

Chapter 8: The Prepared Heart

For Ezra had prepared his heart to seek the Law of the Lord,
and to do it, and to teach statutes and ordinances in Israel.
(Ezra 7:10)

Another type of heart the Bible speaks of is a prepared heart. When I think of something that has been prepared, I think of it as being ready for its intended purpose. The Hebrew word translated as "prepared" is *kun* and it means "set upright, directed, established."[1] This heart is set upright; it is committed to good. It is directed toward the things of God; it has a heavenly focus. This heart is established; it is not led this way and that by feelings, anxieties, distractions, prevalent fads, various doctrines, etc. Such a heart beats for God. And it is ready for God to work within it.

Will You Prepare Your Heart?

In Scripture we read of some people who prepared their hearts to seek and serve the Lord (2 Chron. 19:3, 20:33, 30:19; Job 11:13). Ezra, for example, set his heart to seek, to do, and to teach the Law of God (Ezra 7:10). Hundreds of years later John the baptizer set about *"to make ready a people prepared for the Lord"* (Luke 1:17). Though we live in a different era, we might ask if we are the sort of people who are ready to seek and to serve the Lord, and if we are helping others to be so.

We read of other people in the Scripture who did not prepare their hearts, and sooner or later fell into evil, and were condemned (2 Chron. 12:14). A failure to prepare one's heart before the Lord will lead to sin, while a properly prepared heart will lead a person closer to Him. When looking at the above examples of people with hearts put in order, we see this action is the determination of the inner person prior to a new or renewed seeking after the Lord. It is significant that this action is associated in Scripture with repenting, putting away sin, and committing to look into the Word of God and to do what it says (1 Sam. 7:3; Ezra 7:10).

In the matter of a prepared heart, we see both individual choice and divine intervention. It is appropriate to both pray for God to do a work in one's heart and to take personal action in the matter. As mentioned above, Scripture records many examples of people preparing their own hearts. However, we also read of God Himself preparing hearts (Ps. 10:17, see also 2 Chron. 29:36), and hear others praying for Him to do so (1 Chron. 29:18). This is not at all contradictory. Paul wrote, *"For it is God who works in you both to will and to do for His good pleasure"* (Phil. 2:13). It is God who instills in us the desire to do His will, and who enables us to perform it. We could not call after the Lord unless He first called out to us. Any spiritual growth or ministry must rely on Him. Indeed, this is the very reason our hearts must be prepared.

Humility and the Removal of Idols

Most of us know about preparing a speech, preparing a meal, or preparing for a trip. But how is a heart prepared? I suggest it begins with humility. Hearts are prepared in the same manner that a field is prepared when ground is broken up to ready it for planting. There is a need for brokenness in our lives. Have a heart that receives the Word of God like good ground receives seed and, in time, bears fruit (Luke 8:15). We need to heed the call of Hosea to stiff-necked Israel: *"Sow for yourselves righteousness; reap in mercy; break up your fallow ground, for it is time to seek the Lord, till He comes and rains righteousness on you"* (Hosea 10:12). Another illustration in Scripture of something that needed to be "prepared" is the Levitical offerings that were made ready for sacrifice. The application for us is to relinquish our will, to offer up ourselves as a sacrifice to God – in this way, a heart is prepared for the Lord through brokenness and surrender.

It is also necessary to put away any idols that may have intruded into that sacred place God is to have in one's life. This was the message of the prophet Samuel to the children of Israel:

> *Then Samuel spoke to all the house of Israel, saying, "If you return to the Lord with all your hearts, then **put away the foreign gods** and the Ashtaroths from among you, and **prepare your hearts** for the Lord,*

and serve Him only; and He will deliver you from the hand of the Philistines" (1 Sam. 7:3).

An idol is anything that takes God's rightful position of first place in our life. This means that all of our prized possessions, our goals and occupations, even our closest relationships, need to be a distant second in comparison to our love for the Lord. Let us examine our hearts for idols, and, by God's grace, remove them. God is to be our first love, and there should not be anything in stiff competition!

Having a prepared heart is the *"desire of the humble"* (Ps. 10:17). When we have humbled and submitted ourselves, and have cleansed our hearts from idols – all the while relying on God's working within us – we will then be ready to make a commitment to seek the Lord. As previously mentioned, prepared hearts are frequently associated with the pursuit of God (2 Chron. 12:14, 19:3, 30:19; Ezra 7:10). In the books of Ezra and Job, this is beautifully pictured as stretching out our empty hands to the Lord (Ezra 9:5-6; Job 11:13). Of course, we could never reach God on our own efforts; thankfully, the arm of the Lord is both strong and long, and His hands are stretched out toward us! Just as a seeking Savior and a seeking sinner will find each other, a longing Lord and a longing believer will grow closer together in love and grace. This is why the prophet Isaiah could declare on God's behalf:

> *For thus says the High and Lofty One who inhabits eternity, whose name is Holy: "I dwell in the high and holy place, with him who has a contrite and humble spirit, to revive the spirit of the humble, and to revive the heart of the contrite ones"* (Isa. 57:15).

In conclusion, it is important to note that mere religious reform, apart from properly prepared hearts, is futile (2 Chron. 20:33). It is not trying, but rather dying to self and yielding to God that prepares us to commune with God and to receive His goodness. Self-determination to do better will not produce godliness or anything else that is pleasing to God. The reason a prepared heart is a prerequisite to seeking the Lord is that we will never be close to Him if we do not have a humble attitude, if idols are competing for our love, and if we are not determined to obey what He has revealed to us. God does not force Himself on people. Why should He further reveal Himself to those who have shunned what He has already shown them they must obey? If we want to get serious about our relationship with the Lord, we are going to have to examine our hearts, remove any wrong attitudes or idols from them, and then set them to seek the Lord.

We often have a tinted view of revival as a time of glory and joy and swelling numbers queuing to enter the churches. That is only part of the story. Before the glory and joy, there is conviction; and that begins with the people of God. There are tears of godly sorrow. There are wrongs to put right, secret things...to be thrown out, and bad relationships, hidden for years, to be repaired openly. If we are not prepared for this, we had better not pray for revival.

— Brian Edwards[2]

Chapter 9: The Purposed Heart

*When he came and had seen the grace of God, he was glad, and encouraged
them all that with purpose of heart they should continue with the Lord.*
(Acts 11:23)

The purposed heart is closely associated with the prepared heart.
However, a prepared heart deals mainly with an attitude of readiness,
while this purposed heart focuses on personal resolution, moving
forward into action. A prepared heart is made available for God to use,
while a purposed heart is determined to act on His behalf. In this
context, "prepared" is used as an adjective (e.g. a person with a
prepared heart: Ezra 7:10; Ps. 10:17), whereas "purpose" is more likely
to be found as a verb. For example, Daniel purposed in his heart both to
not defile himself and to understand God's revelation to him (Dan. 1:8,
10:12). Similar expressions are to be found in the New Testament (Acts
11:23; 2 Cor. 9:7).

When Barnabas came to the church at Antioch, his exhortation was
that they would continue with or cleave to the Lord with purpose of
heart. The Greek word used in Acts 11:23 is *prosthesis*, meaning "a
setting forth," or by implication an intention as exposed before God.[1]
The same word is used specifically to speak of how, under the Old
Covenant, the showbread was set before the Lord in the temple (Matt.
12:4; Heb. 9:2). In Acts 11:23 it reflects a heart-offering to the Lord.
We may conclude that a purposed heart is one that is taken and set
before God; it is dedicated, resolute, driven to a fixed intention.

Examples of Purposed Hearts

Let us take a look at some people who had purposed hearts: Ruth,
David, and Daniel. Ruth, a young Moabite widow, resolved to
accompany her mother-in-law back to Israel even though it appeared
she had nothing to gain by doing so, and Naomi herself tried to

45

dissuade her. Ruth was motivated by love for Naomi and an interest in her God. Ruth's courage was remarkable:

> *But Ruth said: "Entreat me not to leave you, or to turn back from following after you; for wherever you go, I will go; and wherever you lodge, I will lodge; your people shall be my people, and your God, my God. Where you die, I will die, and there will I be buried. The Lord do so to me, and more also, if anything but death parts you and me"* (Ruth 1:16-17).

This was an exceptional pledge of devotion. When Naomi saw that Ruth was committed to remaining with her, she said no more to deter her. Ruth did remain with Naomi, identified herself with the Jewish nation, and became a servant of Jehovah. She eventually married Boaz and became a part of the human genealogy of Jesus Christ (Matt. 1:5). It is remarkable what God will do in the lives of those with purposed hearts. The book of Ruth demonstrates His sovereignty and careful workings both in the lives of individuals and in human affairs. No doubt Ruth and Naomi were encouraged by what God did for them in their own time, but they would doubtless have been surprised if they knew how He was operating to bring about His plan of salvation for the human race![2]

King David was a man with a purposed heart. We can see this in his actions (this was the adolescent who stood up against the giant Goliath for the honor of God!), as well as in his writings. One of the psalms he composed, Psalm 101, has been called "A Psalm of Resolution." In it, the words "I will" occur nine times, as David made resolutions regarding his personal life as well as his household and kingdom. These reflections of a purposed heart would be appropriate to apply to our own lives.

As Lee Weber has observed, David first committed himself to sing; it is important for us to rejoice and praise the Lord amid all the changing moods of our lives. He also resolved to behave wisely in a perfect way and to walk with a perfect heart. We must live holy lives before the Lord. If we lack wisdom in how to walk, we should ask Him to supply it (Jas. 1:5). David further purposed not to set anything wicked in front of his eyes. This goes beyond not *doing* sin, to not providing the opportunity for sin. As Paul confirms, believers are to make no provision for our flesh to fulfill its lusts (Rom. 13:14). David determined to have proper companions; carefully evaluate all your relationships (especially friends and close coworkers) and ensure that good morals are not being corrupted by bad companions (1 Cor. 15:33). Finally, David purposed not to tolerate slander, gossip, haughtiness and pride, and deceitfulness. He said he would dispel wickedness from his kingdom *"early"* (v. 8); the purposed heart does not procrastinate! These resolutions are certainly pertinent for our day and time.[3]

Daniel, a young Jewish captive who found himself in the pagan environment of the Babylonian court, purposed in his heart not to defile himself (Dan. 1:8). He was joined in this resolution by three others: Hananiah, Mishael, and Azariah. The test soon came. The king's food was set before them; it is probable that either this food was dedicated to idols, or contained elements contrary to the dietary laws of the Jews, or both. At any rate, the four regarded it as defiling. The *"portion of the king's delicacies"* (v. 8) may be pleasing to the senses, but it is poor food for the soul. Accordingly, Daniel quietly requested that he might not defile himself. He did not "come out swinging" in assumed righteous indignation, nor did he fall into self-pity, doggedly "suffering for righteousness." There are good lessons here for us. Keep yourself *"unspotted from the world"* (Jas. 1:27), but let righteousness be adorned with grace.

Some may question the wisdom of these four young men; they were risking their lives to take this stand; was it really worth it? H. A. Ironside comments on the matter:

> Some who read the account in our day may also consider it all a mere quibble on the part of Daniel, Hananiah, Mishael, and Azariah. But it brings out a principle of great force and beauty that should appeal to every Christian's heart and conscience. The only way to grow in the Lord is by being faithful in little things. He who honors the Lord by conscientious adherence to His Word in what some would call minor details is likely to be exercised about greater things...we may rest assured there are no non-essentials in our Bibles.[4]

Others may say, "It's not *that* bad," but the true heart realizes *anything* that defiles will break the soul's communion with God. It is worth standing up for the "small things" – worth it for the sake of one's own conscience, and worth it also for the testimony the purposed heart conveys to the world.

The Value of a Purposed Heart

These are godly people with hearts that were resolute in the things of God; their actions are recorded in Scripture that we might learn from their example. Let us develop purpose of heart. The first thing that will be helpful in this endeavor is to go to the Word of God. We have already taken a little time to look at Psalm 101; listed below are other verses relating to hearts that are purposed.

We need to ensure that the purposes of our hearts align with God's. Then we have the encouragement of knowing that what the Lord purposes shall be done (Isa. 14:24). Also, when developing purposes of heart, it is good to seek godly counsel (Prov. 15:22, 20:18). It is appropriate for the child of God to form Scriptural resolutions and, by the grace of God, to stand by them. And we are in need of grace: resolutions crafted in holy zeal are often easily broken, as was the case in Nehemiah's day (Neh. 10:29-39, 13:1-31). May we all have purposed hearts and live accordingly!

Biblical Resolutions for the Purposed Heart

- To build God's house (1 Kgs. 5:5)
  (This could be applied, in this dispensation, to a dedication to build up the Church.)
- To not sin with one's mouth (Ps. 17:3)
- To praise and glorify God (Ps. 108:1)
- To trust God (Ps. 112:7-8)
- To not defile oneself (Dan. 1:8)
- To understand God's revelation (Dan. 10:12)
- To give to the Lord (2 Cor. 9:7)
- To cleave to the Lord (Acts 11:23)
- To live out the love of Christ (2 Thess. 3:5)

Chapter 10: The Protected Heart

Keep your heart with all diligence, for out of it spring the issues of life.
(Prov. 4:23)

The human heart weighs less than a pound and is about the size of a person's fist.[1] Yet, each day the average adult heart will beat 104,000 times and pump 8,193 liters of blood; "in terms of work, this is the equivalent of raising 1 ton (907 kg) to a height of 41 feet (12.5 m) every 24 hours."[2] Blood provides life to the cells of the body. Without a functioning heart, you would not live very long at all. As is the case with many facts from the physical realm, the idea that the heart pumps life-sustaining blood is used to illustrate a spiritual truth.

The metaphorical heart is the spiritual center of a person, and from it stem all the issues of life. Matthew Henry writes, "Out of a heart well-kept will flow living issues, good products, to the glory of God and the edification of others"; he then continues, "Our lives will be regular or irregular, comfortable or uncomfortable, according as our hearts are kept or neglected."[3] Whatever is in your heart will spill over into all the other areas of your life: speech, actions, and thoughts (Matt. 12:34-35, 15:18-19). It must, therefore, be strictly watched.

The Fractured Heart

Proverbs 4:23 is frequently applied to "relationships," as we are told to be careful not to bestow pieces of our hearts promiscuously or prematurely, and not to pursue a close relationship with someone we do not intend to marry. While there is both truth and wisdom in this, the meaning of the verse is far more extensive. The issue is that *anything* we have in our hearts **will** affect how we think, act, what we say, and ultimately, who we are. It is easier to deny entrance to an attitude than it is to root it out later. So be very careful of what you **allow** to have a hold in your heart. Matthew Henry explains how our hearts must be kept:

We must maintain a holy jealousy of ourselves, and set a strict guard, accordingly, upon all the avenues of the soul; keep our hearts from doing hurt and getting hurt, from being defiled by sin and disturbed by trouble; keep them as our jewel, as our vineyard; keep a conscience void of offence; keep out bad thoughts; keep up good thoughts; keep the affections upon right objects and in due bounds. *Keep them with all keepings* (so the word is); there are many ways of keeping things – by care, by strength, by calling in help, and we must use them all in keeping our hearts; and all little enough, so deceitful are they, Jer. 17:9. Or *above all keepings;* we must keep our hearts with more care and diligence than we keep anything else. We must keep our eyes (Job 31:1), keep our tongues (Psa. 34:13), keep our feet (Ecc. 5:1), but, above all, keep our hearts.[4]

These days it is popular to be rather reckless with one's heart; the poor things are fragmented and scattered about, spread frightfully thin over a motley assortment of interests. In chapter three we learned the heart is the center of one's personality and involves one's emotions, personal morality, will, and cognition. It is thus prudent to be careful with it.

Guarding a Good Thing

Christ taught: *"A good man out of the good treasure of his heart brings forth good things, and an evil man out of the evil treasure brings forth evil things"* (Matt. 12:35); and again, *"But those things which proceed out of the mouth come from the heart, and they defile a man. For out of the heart proceed evil thoughts, murders, adulteries, fornications, thefts, false witness, blasphemies"* (Matt. 15:18-19). Put up a defensive perimeter around your heart! We want to have hearts that are a treasure trove of good things.

If we are to guard our hearts we must exercise care regarding what makes it into our hearts, that is, on what our gaze lingers and on what our thoughts dwell. Paul writes in the book of Philippians: *"Finally, brethren, whatever things are true, whatever things are noble, whatever things are just, whatever things are pure, whatever things are lovely, whatever things are of good report, if there is any virtue and if there is anything praiseworthy—meditate on these things"* (Phil. 4:8). Do you feel like you need reinforcements in this endeavor to shield your heart? How would you like the peace of God to be on guard duty? Examine the verses which precede the one you just read:

> *Be anxious for nothing, but in everything by prayer and supplication, with thanksgiving, let your requests be made known to God; and **the peace of God**, which surpasses all understanding, **will guard your hearts** and minds through Christ Jesus* (Phil. 4:6-7, emphasis added).

Anxieties are surrendered when a person holds on to God in faith. Oswald Chambers stated, "Faith is deliberate confidence in the character of God whose ways you may not understand at the time."[5] It remembers God's past faithfulness and trusts Him to be faithful in the future; it leads a person to pray and give thanks. This is what we must learn from these verses in Philippians: we are responsible for what we meditate on, and therefore, the direction we allow our heart to take. Meanwhile, we may experience faith, gratitude, contentment, and peace – all through Christ Jesus!

Avoiding Virtual Realities

We are promised grace, and with it peace, for each day, but not for our speculations on imaginary future circumstances. Meditating on such, be it a wish or a worry, is a futile pursuit. A virtual reality we create in our minds is not pleasing to the Lord, for if we do not abide in truth we cannot please the God of Truth; rather, He tells us to think on what is true (Phil. 4:8). Mental pitfalls would include what we might call "mental dating," an activity common among Christian young people who have otherwise "kissed dating goodbye" and outwardly seem committed to avoiding a series of relationships that foster intimacy without commitment.

What are the "symptoms" of the heart disorder of mental dating? Carolyn McCulley writes that these include: going to events just because a certain person will be there, being distracted in church meetings or in the things of God because of him, going home disappointed if he doesn't talk to me, being jealous of the women he does talk to, and ignoring the needs of others around me because of my self-focused mindset.[6]

I refer to this as a "heart disorder" because such mental meanderings hinder spiritual growth and foster abnormal relationships.

They leave the heart unguarded and, ultimately, one's thoughts do affect one's actions. Desire changes to a demand (with expectations of fulfillment), then leads to disappointment. This pattern may also set a person up for disappointment in marriage, and in other relationships and other areas of life, as Paul Tripp explains:

> The objects of most of our desires are not evil. The problem is the way they tend to grow, and the control they come to exercise over our hearts. Desires are a part of human existence, but they must be held with an open hand. ... The problem with desire is that in sinners it very quickly morphs into *demand* ('I must'). Demand is the closing of my fists over a desire. Even though I may be unaware that I have done it, I have left my proper position of submission to God. I have decided that I must have what I have set my heart on and nothing can stand in the way. I am no longer comforted by God's desire for me; I am threatened by it, because God's will potentially stands in the way of my demand. ... There is a direct relationship between expectation and disappointment, and most of our disappointment in relationships is not because people have actually wronged us, but because they have failed to meet our expectations.[7]

Desire, demand, disappointment: who among us has not walked down that road? We would do better to follow the converse pattern found in Philippians 4:6-7: faith, gratitude, contentment, peace – all in Christ Jesus. How might we apply this to the previous scenario of mental dating? We must begin with faith. Have faith in the goodness and power of God; if He wants something to happen in your life, it will, and if He doesn't want it in your life, you would be wise not to want it either. Remember a "prepared heart" wants what God wants. Know He will not withhold anything that is good for you (Ps. 84:11), and He will work everything in your life for good and His glory (Rom. 8:28). Be grateful for the gifts He grants you; name them off one by one, give thanks for them, and see if God doesn't do a work of contentment and peace within your own heart.

Faith, gratitude, contentment, and peace are found in Christ Jesus. This will help defend our hearts against worry, depression, secret idols, empty imaginations and daydreams, unspiritual priorities, and relationships that fail to promote the glory of God. As important as it is to watch over our hearts, it is even more important to direct our gaze at our wonderful Lord, who is so much more worthy of attention than our shabby hearts. The converse danger of an unguarded heart is one that is self-focused, and so we are aptly warned by Robert Murray McCheyne: "Do not take up your time so much with studying your own heart as with studying Christ's heart. For one look at yourself, take ten looks at Christ!"[8] The excellencies of our Lord is a subject we will never exhaust! As we learn of Him, may God fill our hearts with Christ. Spend time considering what His heart is like.

Let your heart be taken up with the Lord Jesus Christ. Guard your own heart by keeping God's Word in your heart (Ps. 119:11), by putting away iniquity, and by having the proper focus and direction. Pray and give thanks; remember the trail we are to blaze through life: faith, gratitude, contentment, and peace (Phil. 4:6-7). As Matthew Henry concludes, "We must keep a watchful eye and a strict hand upon all the motions of our inward man."[9] God furnished you your heart, and with it He also extended to you a solemn charge to keep it with all diligence. Have a protected heart!

I want a godly fear, a quick discerning eye,
That looks to Thee when sin is near and sees the tempter fly;
A spirit still prepared and armed with jealous care,
Forever standing on its guard and watching unto prayer.

I want a true regard, a single, steady aim,
(Unmoved by threatening or reward) to Thee and Thy great Name.
A jealous, just concern for Thine immortal praise;
A pure desire that all may learn and glorify Thy grace.

— Charles Wesley[10]

Part Three

With All Diligence –
Disciplines of the Heart

Chapter 11: Personal Discipline

*But I discipline my body and bring it into subjection, lest, when I
have preached to others, I myself should become disqualified.*
(1 Cor. 9:27)

Before entering the final section of this book, let us revisit Proverbs 4:23, which reads: *"Keep your heart with all diligence, for out of it spring the issues of life."* The *"issues of life"* do indeed proceed from the heart; as we have seen, it is the seat of emotions, character, will, and cognition. In fact, the condition of our heart determines what we are and think and do. We also examined the characteristics of a godly *"heart"* itself. Now, we will look at the middle portion of the verse to see how we should apply *"all diligence"* in regards to the heart. We will examine various disciplines of the heart: self-control, contentment, thankfulness, faithfulness, joy, patience, submission, prayer, and purity. Like disciplined soldiers on an important guard detail, these activities will help us to safeguard our heart in a manner that is honoring to the Lord. Let us consider what discipline is, and why it is needed in our lives.

Are You a Slave?

What sins can you think of that enslave people? Any and every sin can be enslaving, such as stealing, lying, gossip, covetousness, materialism, etc. If you are unable to stop committing a particular sin, then that sin controls you and you are a slave to it. Even things that are not inherently evil can become so if allowed to dominate one's life: the Bible mentions drinking excess wine (Eph. 5:18), but besides substance abuse we might also consider dissipation in the areas of media use, shopping, eating, thought patterns, and so forth. The result of ongoing sin is death, which biblically means separation (Rom. 6:23): for the unregenerate this is eternal condemnation; for the believer, a lack of fellowship with the Lord (Rom. 5:8-16; 1 Jn. 1:6-7).

Are there sins in your life that have enslaved you? Do you feel like a slave to anything other than God? Is anything else controlling you? Paul wrestled with this very issue in Romans 6:11-23, and we find specific encouragements in this passage: Christ died to free me from sin; I am bought by Him, a slave to God; with Him, I am dead to sin and made alive! In Christ, positionally speaking, what I was in Adam is no longer to rule me – it was crucified at the cross (Rom. 6:6-10; Gal. 5:24). Look at the results of sin, and then of a life lived in fellowship with God. Who would you rather have controlling your life? Every soldier of God must take orders from Him, and every disciple of Christ must exercise discipline. We can only serve one master, and Paul exhorts the child of God not to go back to the old master of sin; in Christ we are liberated from sin!

Discipline Defined

The word "discipline" involves "training to act in accordance with rules...activity, exercise, or a regimen that develops or improves a skill."[1] When motivation fails, discipline forges ahead. Some shrink from the thought of discipline, assuming it means foregoing things they enjoy and enduring things they find disagreeable. In reality, the saying holds true; "discipline is choosing what you want most over what you want now." Right *now* I may want to eat an entire carton of Cookies and Cream ice cream, but what I want *more* is to be a healthy weight. So we see that discipline is not forfeiting all you want; it is prioritizing so that you obtain what you know is best. It involves temperance and balance, and it is closely related to self-control. It is not a self-improvement technique and lacks a self-serving appeal, for such things depend on social pressure and personal will-power, which are usually not enough. Elisabeth Elliot simply describes discipline as "placing oneself under orders."[2] For the Christian, discipline is not just choosing what we want most, but rather aligning our wants with what God wants most for us. He has the best plan for our lives, after all!

While people often have negative connotations of discipline and self-control, taking these to mean only punishment or something generally unpleasant, in truth, both of these virtues lead to liberty. For example, I do not have the freedom to play a beautiful piece on the violin as my sister has, because I never had the discipline to practice it as she has over the years. The disciplined life is one that is equipped and enabled for action and productivity. Those who strive for mastery are temperate in all things, lest they be mastered (1 Cor. 9:24-27).

Its Reason, Focus, Work, and Hope

Scripture reveals the reason, focus, work, and hope of discipline. The **reason** we are to be disciplined is founded in the remembrance of God's grace and Christ's sacrifice (Titus 2:11-14). How can we lead lives of frivolity after He has done so much to supply us with His abundant life?

The **focus** of a disciplined life needs to be God Himself (Gal. 5:16-26); this is the "secret" to spiritual success: abide in Christ and allow God to have His way in you and the Holy Spirit to produce spiritual fruit in you. If we live in the Spirit, let us walk in the Spirit, and if we walk in the Spirit, we shall not fulfill the lusts of the flesh. We have fellowship with the Father when we are not living in unconfessed sin (1 John 1:3-6). Fellowship with the Father, abiding in Christ, and walking in the Spirit are expressions of the same reality: our communion with God. It is important, when exercising discipline, to make neither sin nor ourselves our point of concentration – our eyes must be fixed on God!

Discipline's **work** is to exercise ourselves unto godliness, as Paul exhorted his spiritual son Timothy: *"exercise yourself toward godliness. For bodily exercise profits a little, but godliness is profitable for all things, having promise of the life that now is and of that which is to come"* (1 Tim. 4:7b-8). The Greek word *gumnazō* translated "exercise" in this passage[3] is the same root word from which we get our English word "gymnasium," and this imagery tells us something of the discipline involved in the pursuit of godliness. Remember this *"is profitable for all things."*

The Bible gives us further specific instructions that will assist us in this work (Titus 2:11-14; 1 Pet. 1:13, 4:7, 5:8):

- Deny ungodliness and worldly lusts.
- Prepare your mind for action, ridding it of clutter.
- Watch for the adversary's wiles, watch unto prayer, and watch for the Lord's return.
- Be sober, that is, self-controlled, rational, balanced, and without frivolity.

The **hope** of self-discipline is Christ's coming, when we shall be like Him (1 Jn. 3:2; Titus 2:11-14). When we see Christ, we will no longer need to wrestle with ourselves. The course will be over, the battle will be won, and discipline will have served its purpose. But apart from discipline it is likely that we will be ashamed at His coming (1 Jn. 2:28).

The Disciplined Life

In summary, let us consider the characteristics of a disciplined life. The self-disciplined woman is in control of her thoughts, emotions, speech, and actions. She is not brought under the power of any enslaving thing; she has the perception to see areas of possible bondage and the good sense to avoid them. Though it can be said that she controls herself, in reality she is a slave to God. By this she is: dead to sin and alive to God; free from sin and a slave to God; characterized by obedience, righteousness, holiness, and submission to God. The self-disciplined woman is motivated to avoid sin because she knows it will sever her communion with the God she loves. She is eternally-minded and looks for Christ's return. She keeps Christ's travail for her in mind. Her life is grounded, focused on God. She actively exercises herself unto godliness by: denying sin and worldly lusts, preparing her mind for action, watching for the adversary's deceitful tricks, watching unto prayer, and watching for the Lord's return. She has clear priorities: the eternal takes precedence over the temporal, the spiritual comes before the physical, and people are more important than things.

Note the importance of discipline. If you allow yourself to lose control, you will lose effectiveness in your service to God. You may bring derision to God's name. You may stumble other believers. You may be an excuse for unbelievers to reject the gospel. You will bring the chastening hand of God upon you. Watch – don't lose your testimony!

Know that you will be swimming against the tide; discipline is not a popular concept these days (2 Tim. 3:3). The world, the flesh, and the devil will all be against you on this one. But when you say "yes" to God, He provides you with the power to live a disciplined life for Him (1 Cor. 10:13). This is a principle we see throughout Scripture: what He commands, He enables us to do; those who submit to Him, He will uphold in righteousness. As Paul the apostle said, *"If God is for us, who can be against us?"* (Rom. 8:31). Let us go forward in His strength.

If we're living for the same world that everyone else is, we'll never convince them to live for another.

— J. B. Nicholson[4]

Chapter 12: The Discipline of Self-Control

Do you not know that those who run in a race all run, but one
receives the prize? Run in such a way that you may obtain it.
And everyone who competes for the prize is temperate in all things.
(1 Cor. 9:24-25a)

In the previous chapter, we discovered that discipline is willingly placing oneself under orders. For the Christian, it means making God's priorities our priorities and then choosing what is the most beneficial over what we want now. It brings focus and productivity to our lives. It includes the virtue of self-control, which is "the ability to exercise restraint or control over one's feelings, emotions, reactions, etc."[1] In this chapter, we will look at how self-control needs to be specifically exercised in the following areas of our lives: thoughts, emotions, speech, and behavior. Self-control is a powerful tool when it comes to keeping our hearts with all diligence.

Self-control – is it possible? Can you channel your energy, control yourself, and say "no" to your flesh? No, not really; that is, you cannot do it by yourself. However, self-control is a fruit of the Spirit (Gal. 5:22-23). Like the rest of the fruit of the Spirit, He develops self-control in our lives as we abide in Him and submit to Him. We cannot create self-control no matter how hard we try, but God can (and will) produce this in us as we choose to actively die to self. Self-control is not the same as the "self-help" message we hear so much of these days; it is *Spirit-control*. It is not enough to not be under the control of wine, etc.; we need to be under the control of the Holy Spirit (Eph. 5:18). You will always be a slave of sorts (that is just how it is), but you can choose by what or by whom you will be mastered. Will you be a slave to sin, or a slave to Christ? Whose will are you fulfilling (see 2 Tim. 2:26; Rom. 6:11-23)? If you're not doing the will of God, you're honoring the will of the devil (Eph. 5:14-17). In the candid words of Nancy Rolinger, "Maybe you like being the one who's in control of your life, but frankly, if you're in control of your life, you're going to blow it!"[2] True freedom and fulfillment is found in submission to Christ, as King Solomon discovered in the book of Ecclesiastes.

The Spirit-Controlled Life

Before we examine specific areas in which to exercise self-control, let us first consider a few general points in regards to living the Spirit-controlled life. Romans 13:13 describes various sins that result from a lack of self-control, while the following verse gives us a two-part strategy we can use to confront these: we are to put on Christ and to make no provision for the flesh.

First, put on Christ (Rom. 13:14a). To do this, one must have the mindset of reporting for duty as an undistracted soldier (2 Tim. 2:4). Be in Scripture; this is not a matter of "check-the-box-got-my-Word-of-God-shot-for-the-day." Rather, let the Word of God dwell in you richly and have its way with you (Col. 3:16). The Bible is our instruction book (Jer. 35:13), our light (Ps. 119:105), our food (Ps. 119:103). (Do you read your Bible as often as you eat? Do you meditate on it as long as it takes your body to digest your physical food?) Be in prayer. Eschew evil. Paul could summarize his life with one word, "Christ" (Phil. 1:21); might this be said of us?

Second, make no provision for the flesh (Rom. 13:14b). Know your weaknesses and do not feed them (Col. 3:5). Guess what happens when you do not feed the flesh nature? It shrivels up and its influence will continue to die! If there is a stumbling stone in your path heavenward, get rid of it! Do not coddle sin – cut it off (put it to death; see Rom. 8:13; Col. 3:5). In some areas, you win the battle by running away from the conflict, as did Joseph in the house of Potiphar. The Bible instructs us to turn and flee from: immorality (1 Cor. 6:18), idolatry (1 Cor. 10:14), youthful lusts (2 Tim. 2:22), discontentment and covetousness (1 Tim. 6:11). On the other hand, we have the encouragement from James 4:7 that if we resist the devil by standing fast in the truth, he will flee from us.

To summarize, the Spirit-controlled life will have two actions: putting off and putting on; this might be called "the remove and replace strategy." If there is an area in your life in which you do not have the control you should, remove the offending behavior and replace it with a Christlike behavior. This is what it means to put off the deeds of the flesh and to put on Christ (Col. 3:7-14). For example, if you are spending too much time on the internet, use that time to memorize Scripture instead. If you are spending too much money on yourself, give to others instead. One cannot merely stop a pattern of thought and/or behavior – something always comes to fill up the empty places. Ensure what fills up the spaces in your mind and heart and life is Christlike. Put on Christ!

Gird Your Mind

The general strategy just discussed may be applied to the various areas of our lives in which self-control, or *Spirit-control*, is needed: thoughts, emotions, speech, and behavior. Let us now take a brief look at each of these and see what practical applications may be made. Did you know we are responsible for our thought life? As we learned in chapter six, we serve a God so holy that He views hatred as murder (1 Jn. 3:15), lust as adultery (Matt. 5:28), and covetousness as idolatry (Col. 3:5). Sins of the mind are still sins. It behooves us to exercise self-control in this area: *"And do not be conformed to this world, but be transformed by the renewing of your mind, that you may prove what is that good and acceptable and perfect will of God"* (Rom. 12:2). We literally are to be *metamorphosed* by the *renovation* of the mind. Sometimes the material world dominates our thinking; beware, because our thoughts influence who we are: *"For as he thinks in his heart, so is he"* (Prov. 23:7a). Therefore, *"Set your mind on things above, not on things on the earth"* (Col. 3:2). Let the ideas of heaven, eternity, God's Word, God's work, and God Himself abide in your mind; let them be the things to which your thoughts ever return.

Peter the apostle instructs us: *"Therefore, gird up the loins of your mind..."* (1 Pet. 1:13a). In Biblical times when men wore long, flowing robes, it was common to *"gird up the loins"* before hard labor by belting in the lower hem around the waist. Any woman who has worn a full-length skirt, dress, or formal gown understands how much easier it would be to run, work in muddy fields, etc. without a long robe around one's ankles! The application for us is not to hike up our hemlines, but rather to be unhindered in our thinking, ready for action by getting what is not necessary out of the way. Someone who girded his robe also kept it from getting dirty, and we might consider how having a "girded" mind helps keep us from defilement. This mind is unsullied, focused, neither overwhelmed nor anxious, and ready for action.

In confronting an attack of false teachers, Paul provides instructions regarding a victorious thought life:

> *For though we walk in the flesh, we do not war according to the flesh. For the weapons of our warfare are not carnal but mighty in God for pulling down strongholds, casting down arguments and every high thing that exalts itself against the knowledge of God, bringing every thought into captivity to the obedience of Christ* (2 Cor. 10:3-5).

The Christian does not wage war with guns, modern stratagems, power, wealth, or diplomatic fluency. Instead, he or she uses spiritual weapons such as the Word of God, faith and the rest of the armor of God, and prayer (Eph. 6:13-18), as well as righteousness (2 Cor. 6:7). These are used to tear down reasonings, beliefs, and philosophies that are contrary to the teachings of the Lord Jesus Christ.

In this endeavor, the Christian would be wise to first see there are no strongholds in his or her own mind. Such fortifications come in many shapes, and some are difficult to detect. In one person may lie a craggy buttress of bitterness, in another a fierce citadel of greed, in another a black hold of envy, and in another a slovenly keep of self-pity. Such things are contrary to the knowledge of God, and every thought must be brought captive to Christ. The Christian must put on Christ and make no provision for the flesh. Watch the eye and ear gates to the mind! If a bad thought or manner of thinking comes into your mind, kick it out and replace it with something Christ-honoring. Your mind will never be empty, so it is important to occupy it with good. As the children's song states:

> Don't let your mind go awandering, awandering, on sinful things;
> Don't let your mind go awandering – concentrate on godly things!
> When Satan comes to tempt you with a thought you know is wrong,
> Replace it with the Word of God, a Scripture, or a song.
> Don't let your mind go awandering – concentrate on godly things![3]

Beware of wandering thoughts; have a mind that is stayed on Christ. Consider memorizing specific, relevant spiritual songs or Bible verses to turn to when certain thoughts come; prayer is always a good alternative as well. Concentration is a discipline. It must be practiced.

Direct Your Emotions

Let us next consider how self-control is necessary with emotions. Nancy Rolinger poses the challenge: "Examine your emotional life. Do you live on the feeling level of life? Are you out of control emotionally?"[4] If exercising control over one's thought life sounded difficult, this seems so much harder! Are emotions really things we can control? In her book, *Discipline: The Glad Surrender*, Elisabeth Elliot probes:

> Are we to be mere victims of our feelings, like boats adrift without sail or rudder or anchor? Are we really at their mercy? If it feels good, we do it; if it doesn't, we don't – is that how the disciple is meant to live? Is that discipline?[5]

It certainly does not sound like discipline. Recall that the Bible speaks of *"prepared hearts,"* which means these are "set upright, directed, established."[6] From this we recognize that we are responsible for the direction of our hearts. With the understanding that it is important for us to guide our hearts, note that we are told, not to *feel* thankful, but to give thanks. We are instructed, not to *feel* happy, but to rejoice; and we are taught, not to *feel* "spiritual," but to continue praising and praying to God. We are supposed to steer our hearts, rather than being controlled by them. It is not so much about what emotions you have as it is what you do with them.

In one of her talks on the discipline of emotions, Elisabeth Elliot stated, "Feelings, like thoughts, must be brought into captivity."[7] A puzzled young woman approached her later to inquire how she herself had gotten rid of her own feelings. Elisabeth Elliot reflects:

> Woe is me. Had I failed to explain that I was not talking about *getting rid* of feelings? Did she think I had reached some high spiritual plane where only the mind and spirit operated and feelings were extinct? I went over it again: as long as we live in the "body of this death" we shall struggle against the lower nature, against that which is always at war with God. The "evil that I would not" is still there. Feelings are strong, whether good ones or bad ones. Sometimes they help,

67

sometimes they hinder. It is *discipline* we are discussing. If we are talking about disciplining a racehorse or a child, we are not talking about getting rid of either, but rather bringing them under control.[8]

We must put on Christ; in the Gospels we always see Christ in control of His emotions, not controlled by them, even strong emotions such as anger (e.g. Ps. 78:38; Matt. 21:12-13). Search the Word of God to learn about appropriate emotions. Make no provision for the flesh; know what "pushes your buttons" and try to avoid, or at least set a guard against, these triggers! Search the Word of God to evaluate bad emotions. Curb your emotions to fit God's Word: "*Guide your heart in the way*" (Prov. 23:19). Do not be led by your heart – you must lead your heart.

Scripture does indeed have much to say on the subject of emotions, including ones that are often difficult to control, such as anger and anxiety. We know those who are slow to wrath have great understanding, while those with a hasty spirit exhibit folly (Prov. 14:29). It is often discrete, even a quiet glory, to let go of anger (Prov. 19:11). Another proverb states, "*He who is slow to anger is better than the mighty, and he who rules his spirit than he who takes a city*" (Prov. 16:32). Anger is not a sin in itself – there are some things about which we would do well to be angry – but anger should always serve a present, righteous purpose, and the emotion should never control the person.

Another emotion that is easy to get out of hand is anxiety (consider Phil. 4:6). Christ instructed His disciples on the eve of His crucifixion, "*Let not your heart be troubled; you believe in God, believe also in Me*" (John 14:1). Ann Voscamp reflects on this verse, "Stress isn't only a joy stealer. The way we respond to it can be sin…Trust, it's the antithesis of stress. 'Oh, the joys of those who trust the Lord' (Ps. 40:4)."[9] Stressful things will happen, but when they do, we should not permit stress to steal our joy. Trusting impedes stressing and is just what God requires of us (e.g. John 6:29). Anxiety may seem easier, but we need the discipline to dismiss it in favor of trust. Ann Voscamp continues, "If authentic, saving belief is the act of trusting, then to choose stress is an act of disbelief…atheism. *Anything less than gratitude and trust is practical atheism.*"[10] Whenever I say "I'm stressed out," what I'm really saying is "I'm not trusting God," and, though a child of God, I am acting like an atheist. I would say that stress, like anger, is not a sin in itself, but the way we respond to it can be sinful. Being controlled by unrighteous anger or being "stressed out" can both cause real physical damage to a person, and these can also affect a person's ability to function and relate to other people in his or her life. (It is understood there are various causes for anxiety or depression, but presently we are considering what we can resolve through changes in our attitudes. Disciples of Christ with disciplined thinking will minimize the non-organic triggers of anxiety in their lives. Anchoring one's mind in truth is also one step towards helping a person who suffers from an anxiety disorder.)

However, ignoring negative thoughts and attitudes is usually less than effective; these tend to forever be popping back up from the background of our minds, nagging and affecting our decisions. The psalmists were honest about their feelings and poured out their hearts to the Lord (see Ps. 62:8). This is the appropriate method of action: *"Casting all your care upon Him, for He cares for you"* (1 Pet. 5:7); bring your cares to God and *leave* them with Him!

We see the psalmists, while they honestly expressed their feelings to God, still praised Him. We always have reasons for praise, thanksgiving, worship, and joy! This is part of putting on Christ and making no provision for the flesh; it is the same "remove and replace" strategy. As Ann Voscamp states, "You can't positive-think your way out of negative feelings...Feelings work faster than thoughts ...The only way to fight a feeling is with a feeling."[11] We must be intentional about our emotions to insure these are based in truth and are God-honoring. Praise God for who He is, what He has done, and what He gives. Often this will bring peace and joy, but even if emotional calm eludes you, still you can function by proceeding out of obedience to God. Don't let wrong emotions lead your actions; let right actions transform your emotions. Your feelings may be less than ideal, but you do not have to be "enslaved" by them!

Govern Your Speech

Our speech is another area in which we must exercise self-control. May this be our prayer: *"Let the words of my mouth and the meditation of my heart be acceptable in Your sight, O Lord, my strength and my Redeemer"* (Ps. 19:14). I say a lot of negative things. Often these are in jest, but even so, they are hardly things the Lord or a serious disciple of the Lord would say. Moreover, Proverbs tells us that voicing something cutting to another person, but quickly covering it with the (modernly-translated) phrase, "Just kidding!" is *"like a madman who throws firebrands, arrows, and death..."* (Prov. 26:18-19). Such barbs may seem innocuous enough, but are actually very destructive. I have learned it is wholly unnecessary to express the majority of this negativity, and so I will pray: *"Set a guard, O Lord, over my mouth; keep watch over the door of my lips"* (Ps. 141:3). When it is necessary to provide unfavorable feedback, the timing must be right, our motives must be pure, and truth must be swaddled with love. Also take care your words proceed from a discerning heart and not a critical one; often the difference is marked by tears, that is, our brokenness (2 Cor. 2:4; Phil. 3:18).

It is not only the outright evil words we must watch, but idle words as well. Christ stated, *"But I say to you that for every idle word men may speak, they will give account of it in the day of judgment"* (Matt. 12:36). That is sobering. The Greek word translated here as "idle" means unemployed or useless.[12] Let us consider how many of our words are a waste of time, and employ our speech in a meaningful way.

Nancy Rolinger offers the following advice: "Restrain your desire to express yourself (Prov. 29:11). Listen to others rather than speak (Jas. 1:19). Don't blow up and vent (Prov. 16:32)."[13] The skill of listening is one that always merits improvement. Not listening is indicative of pride, selfishness, and the desire to express oneself (which the Bible calls foolish, Prov. 29:11). Another proverb states: *"The one who guards his mouth preserves his life; the one who opens wide his lips comes to ruin"* (Prov. 13:3, NASB). Put on Christ: He always spoke the truth, and His words were always gracious. Do not offer an opportunity to your flesh: know what your weaknesses are. Perhaps there are certain situations (e.g. group chatter, late-night-sleep-deprived conversations) of which you ought to be wary? Paul instructed the Ephesians, *"Let no corrupt speech proceed out of your mouth, but such as is good for edifying as the need may be, that it may give grace to them that hear"* (Eph. 4:29, ASV). Remove and replace! Speak of and for the Lord. Brian Gunning remarks:

There is never a right time for a wrong word. And there is sometimes a wrong time for even a right word. Make an effort to communicate encouragement. Best we keep our tongues busy speaking the right word. Otherwise they get busy otherwise.[14]

They will certainly be busy otherwise. Let us commit to having *Spirit-controlled* speech!

Control Your Behavior

There is a tie between physical and spiritual discipline; as Elisabeth Elliot says, "We cannot give our hearts to God and keep our bodies for ourselves."[15] It is hard to imagine a serious disciple who is undisciplined in the amount and type of food eaten, inconsistent in physical exercise, and disorderly in personal hygiene and appearance. Naturally, the specifics of such self-discipline will vary from person to person, but it is difficult to be self-controlled in spiritual things if one has not learned self-control in these lesser matters. One's aim in caring for these is not to feel better about oneself or to look better to other people, but to be self-disciplined for the glory of God, and as physically fit as possible for His service (though He has called many to serve in illness or weakness).

You can tell a lot about the spiritual state of people by looking at two things: their bank statements and their daily planners. These reveal what a person does with his or her money and time. Are you a good steward of the material resources God has entrusted to you? The New Testament does not charge Christians with the command to tithe that the Israelites were given in the Old Testament: rather, as William MacDonald wrote, "It is a privilege to give. The question is not: How much must I give? But how much may I sacrifice."[16] Christ has given us everything; how much can we afford to keep for ourselves? Here are some biblical principles concerning the subject of giving to the Lord.

We learn from 1 Corinthians 16:1-4 that giving should be *regular*, not sporadic; Paul exhorted the Corinthians to set aside money on a weekly basis (Sundays), preventing offerings that were emotionally-driven, haphazard, or spasmodic. From this passage we also see that funds should also be handled with accountability (a plural number of people were to oversee the distribution of this gift to the saints at

71

Jerusalem); consider how your gift will be used and be sensible about where you put your money.

Other portions of Scripture inform us that our giving to the Lord should be *proportional* – as God *"prospers"* the individual (Acts 11:29; Mark 12:43-44); however, we should also consider the example of the Macedonians (2 Cor. 8:2), who in their deep poverty yet gave richly. Giving should be done *cheerfully*, *bountifully*, and *purposefully* (2 Cor. 9:6-8). It must be of a *free will* (2 Cor. 8:3, 12), and it must be *sacrificial* (2 Cor. 8:2; Heb. 13:16). Giving should be done *quietly*; others should not know what you are doing, and you yourself should not keep before you a record of your generosity (Matthew 6:1-4). Finally, it is important to give *wisely*, as a good steward (we are called to wisdom: Eph. 5:15; Col. 1:9). Giving is an investment for eternity (Luke 16:9). God multiplies the blessings (2 Cor. 9:8-14); consider the example of the boy who gave the five loaves and two fishes to the Lord. Christ takes our not-enough and makes it enough-and-more!

> A man there was, some did count him mad,
> The more he cast away, the more he had.

> — John Bunyan[17]

Be committed to *giving* extravagantly instead of *living* extravagantly. Put on Christ. We follow the One who had nowhere to lay His head (Matt. 8:20), and who did not carry a denarius (Matt. 22:19). Make no provision for the flesh; before you buy something, ask yourself if there is a better use of your money. Be intentional in your giving.

We have considered whether our bank statements show we are disciples of Christ; now, what is the testimony of our daily planners? George Müller stated, "Wasting time is unbecoming a saint who is bought by the precious blood of Jesus. His time and all that he has is to be used for the Lord."[18] Consider the difference between what seems urgent and what is important. From the moment we wake each morning, the urgent comes upon us like a storm: there are things to do, places to go, people to see! The urgent often distracts us from what is truly important, the things of eternal value. Watching television and movies, surfing the internet, interacting through social media, and reading books may have their place, but if anything takes your time, energy, or affection away from God, it is idolatry (Hos. 2:13). Paul tells us, *"But she that lives in habits of self-indulgence is dead while living"* (1 Tim. 5:6, Darby). Take care; do not label as "entertainment" what God calls "sin." Keep to the unentangled life described in 2 Timothy 2:4; this means we do not allow the world to entangle and strangle us with things.

Put on Christ. We read of Him in prayer and in ministry. It is to be highly doubted whether He spent much time at all in personal respite or repose. Structure your time to reflect the priorities of knowing God and making Him known. Read, pray, meditate, praise, worship, serve. Make no provision for the flesh; do not waste time on things that do not count! And do not let even your service for the Lord come before your personal time with Him. The work of the Lord must not distract us from the Lord of the work.

Full Jurisdiction

Along with our thoughts, emotions, and speech, the Spirit must be allowed full jurisdiction of our behaviors. Take an honest look at your life to see what behaviors need to be brought under control. Whether this be eating, accumulating stuff or prestige, reading material, television programs, online networking, social activities, use of time, use of money, etc. Do not permit your flesh nature to have its way (Rom. 13:14). Replace wrong behavior with right behavior (Eph. 4:22-32); say "no" to self (Matt. 16:24).

Does this work of self-control sound difficult? It would be impossible on our own. However, God is ever so much more committed to self-control in the lives of His children than we are. He has given us all things to live a life of godliness according to His divine power (2 Pet. 1:3-4). As we submit to Him, He conforms us to His own image. Let us not resist this crucial work by a lack of discipline! When our minds are controlled by our spirit, as enabled by the Holy Spirit, our heart will be properly guided in the way it should go and out of it will flow good issues of life.

Seven Areas That Reveal the Quality of Our Spiritual Health:
- What we want the most
- What we think about the most
- How we use our money
- What we do with our leisure time
- The company we enjoy
- Whom and what we admire
- What we laugh at

— A. W. Tozer[19]

Chapter 13: The Discipline of Contentment

Complete in Thee, each want supplied,
And no good thing to me denied;
Since Thou my portion, Lord, will be
I ask no more, complete in Thee.
(Aaron R. Wolfe)[1]

If you tried to visualize the word "contentment," what would come to mind? Often we think of a life at rest, without need or pressing circumstances: perhaps a seaside hammock or a mountain cabin! In fact, contentment is a state of mind that arises from one's inward disposition, and not from external situations. Easton's 1897 Bible Dictionary offers this definition:

[Contentment] is the offspring of humility, and of an intelligent consideration of the rectitude and benignity of divine providence (Ps. 96:1,2, 145:1-21), the greatness of the divine promises (2 Pet. 1:4), and our own unworthiness (Gen. 32:10); as well as from the view the gospel opens up to us of rest and peace hereafter (Rom. 5:2).[2]

As such, contentment is dependent upon one's attitude, not one's circumstances. In fact, Paul said he had learned to be content, regardless of situation:

Not that I speak in regard to need, for I have learned in whatever state I am, to be content: I know how to be abased, and I know how to abound. Everywhere and in all things I have learned both to be full and to be hungry, both to abound and to suffer need. I can do all things through Christ who strengthens me (Phil. 4:11-13).

Have you learned to be content in whatever state you find yourself: in abundance or in need, at home or away, employed or unemployed, single or married? God orders the events of our lives; are you being faithful to all that He has for you to learn and do and enjoy in your current position?

Are You a Complainer?

Do you have a content heart or a complaining heart? To complain is to verbally express doubt in God; it is saying, "God, you're not *good* enough. You're not *wise* enough. You're not *powerful* enough. *You* are not enough." One test of contentment is how we feel when others receive blessings we would like to have: do we rejoice with them, or hide a bitter heart behind a superficial smile and words of congratulations?

Recall the Parable of the Laborers and the Parable of the Forgiven Debtor. In the first (Matt. 20:1-16), a householder went out early in the morning and hired some men who agreed to toil all day in his vineyard for a denarii (the typical day's wage for unskilled labor). The householder later found men at nine, noon, three, and five who agreed to work what remained of the day for whatever wages the householder deemed right. In the end, all received a full day's wage, regardless of the time they started. The initial group of laborers were upset about this, but the householder explained that he had not wronged them: they had received what they had agreed to – a fair day's wage! It was not their place to be offended because he had shown grace to the others. Thus, when I see others being blessed, I ought to rejoice in the demonstration of God's goodness, also knowing He will never be unfair to me.

In the second parable (Matt. 18:23-35), a king found a man who owed him 10,000 talents, an enormous sum of money. In mercy, he responded to the man's plea and canceled his entire debt. However, after receiving such mercy, the same man went out and found a man who owed him only 100 denarii and violently demanded that the other pay him what was owed, and had him cast into prison when unable to do so. When the king heard of this, he sharply rebuked the man, saying, *"should you not also have had compassion on your fellow-servant, just as I had pity on you?"* (Matt. 18:33). The man was in turn thrown into prison until he could pay *his* original debt, which was 600,000 times greater than the debt he was unwilling to forgive. The lesson is this: how can we be unhappy about the blessings God bestows to others when He has already given us so much?

Are You Content?

The previously mentioned statement from Philippians regarding contentment in all things is challenging. Yet Paul immediately follows it by revealing the source of his strength: *"I have strength for all things in Him that gives me power"* (Phil. 4:13, Darby). The ability to lead a life of contentment comes from the Lord Jesus Christ. As such, contentment makes no sense to the natural man. And even believers, if they are living according to the flesh, will find it difficult to trust in the Lord when they are in lack; (they will equally find it hard to rely on Him when they are not). We need spiritual strength to enjoy a settled disposition despite external challenges.

In fact, the flesh nature is never content – it always wants more! While not all of its desires are negative, lusting for what is outside the will of God is wrong. God created us with mechanisms to keep us alive, healthy, and procreative. For example, if my stomach is growling at me, it is not wrong to satisfy its desire for food, yet eating more than I need is wrong because gluttony is outside of God's plan for me. Therefore, we are told to mortify the deeds of the flesh, that is, not to long for and pursue what is beyond God's will. What I have is what God wants me to have, and I should be content. If there is a legitimate need, I am to submit it to the Lord without complaining and remember that my joy is in the Lord, not in earthly things.

Our hearts belong with our treasure in heaven, not buried in the moldering things of earth. The Bible includes many exhortations to contentment. Paul urged, *"And having food and clothing, with these we shall be content"* (1 Tim. 6:8). The words here indicate that we should be satisfied with sustenance and covering. When a group of soldiers asked John the baptizer what they should do, he told them *"...be content with your wages"* (Luke 3:14b). The writer of Hebrews clarifies, *"...be content with such things as you have..."* and quickly follows the exhortation with a reminder that we have the promise of the continual presence of God (Heb. 13:5) – surely all believers can be content with this!

Discontent is destructive. We see this in the history of Israel. In the book of Jeremiah, one of the reasons God lists for the coming destruction of Judah is: *"Because from the least of them even to the greatest of them, everyone is given to covetousness; and from the prophet even to the priest, everyone deals falsely"* (Jer. 6:13). Their covetous nature seemed to be associated with their reprehensible behavior and resistance to God's Word. They rejected divine truth (which is what they really needed for life), and coveted what they did not have and what, in the overall scheme of things, would not make their life better. This highlights a principle for us: covetousness is a matter of wrong perspective, looking away from what is important to concentrate on what is not. If we continue to ponder all that God has graciously granted us – particularly His Word, His promises, and His presence – this is a safeguard against coveting for what we do not have (and likely do not need). Peter writes, *"As His divine power has given to us all things that pertain to life and godliness, through the knowledge of Him who called us by glory and virtue"* (2 Pet. 1:3). God has already given us all we truly require; let us thank Him for these blessings!

Are You Appropriately Discontent?

With that said, note there are times not to be content. It was inappropriate, for example, for Joshua to lapse into despair after the first battle of Ai ended in defeat and to cry that the Hebrews should have been content to stay on the far side of the Jordan River (Josh. 7:7). They had been slaves in Egypt, and God had brought them out by His power and had commanded them to enter the Promised Land! In matters such as these, where God's will is clear, simple obedience is the appropriate response. You should not be content with your level of spiritual growth, especially if you are ignoring God's will. And you do not have to wait to "feel led" when God has commanded you to move forward.

Take a moment to look at the life of Paul. An apostle, missionary, well-known preacher, well-educated Jew, he was not content to remain where he was, spiritually speaking. Instead, he resolved, *"Not that I have already attained, or am already perfected: but I press on, that I may lay hold of that for which Christ Jesus has also laid hold of me"* (Phil. 3:12). We should, like Paul, lay aside our hindrances and press forward toward the high calling of God in Christ Jesus (Phil. 3:13-14; Heb. 12:1). C. H. Spurgeon said, "Self-satisfaction is the grave of progress."[3] We are to be content with what God provides us and where He places us, but we should never be content with failure to do what God says or stagnation in our own spiritual growth.

78

Taking Action Against Discontentment

Paul apprised Timothy, *"Now godliness with contentment is great gain"* (1 Tim. 6:6). A contented disposition will adorn the Christian faith. Are you willing to make a deliberate choice to be content? This will require self-discipline to take personal action against three manifestations of discontentment: covetousness, self-pity, and depression.

First, we are instructed, *"Therefore **put to death** your members which are on the earth: fornication, uncleanness, passion, evil desire, and **covetousness, which is idolatry"*** (Col. 3:5). Note that covetousness is equated with idolatry. This is because it puts something or someone before God in our affections and thoughts, to the point that pursuit of what is coveted displaces our pursuit of God and what He desires for us. For this reason, covetousness is not to be tolerated; we are commanded to mortify it from our lives. The word "mortify" comes from the Greek word *nekroo*, which figuratively means "to deprive of strength," but its literal meaning is "to make dead."[4] Thankfulness is a useful weapon for killing discontentment. If you believe you are lacking something, evaluate the matter from a spiritual perspective, optimize and be thankful for what you do have, and commit the rest to prayer, but do not fall to discontentment. Remember that at this present moment the Lord has given you exactly what He wants you to have. In the next chapter, we will examine the subject of thankfulness more fully.

Another manifestation of discontentment is self-pity, and this one is an ugly monster. It is to feel sorry for oneself, typically when there is little for which to be sorry. It broods on imaginations and loses contact with reality. It prevents us from feeling compassion for others, and cuts off our interactions with other people. It is a lonely, gloomy, all-absorbing pleasure. Yes, pleasure – the flesh loves to pity itself. How does one win the victory over this fiend? We must take our attention off of self and focus it onto Christ, and then others. When you start to feel sorry for yourself, turn your thoughts to God, His Word, His promises, and what is truly important in life. Also, focus your mind on the needs of others and how you can serve them. This will help to prevent you from falling into the trap of self-pity.

Another way discontentment can manifest itself is in depression. (I refer to the emotion, not the clinical disorder.) Even spiritual heroes are vulnerable to this weakness, as we can see in the life of Elijah. Shortly after the powerful showdown against the prophets of Baal on Mt. Carmel, we find Elijah alone in a desert cave (1 Kgs. 18-19). Why? Jezebel had placed a death threat upon him, yet this was no new thing for the prophet of God. It seems he got plain discouraged when a nationwide repentance did not result from Jehovah's clear demonstration of divine power. Elijah isolated himself, fell into self-pity, and lost touch with reality (he claimed he was the only one who served God, but Obadiah had previously told him that he was hiding 100 godly prophets from the queen, and God informed him that there were 7,000 in Israel who hadn't bowed to Baal). Elijah had a difficult ministry, and he wanted to be done.

Warren Henderson observes, "What brought Elijah's ministry to a close? It was his own mental disposition toward the faithfulness of God. He weighed the events of the day according to his own expectations for his ministry and was unsatisfied and thus entered into spiritual depression."[5] We can safeguard our hearts from depression by refusing to set expectations for our ministries; be faithful to what God assigns you to do and trust Him with the results. This side of heaven, none of us can see the full fruit of a ministry; success cannot be measured by visible results. If we have done His will with contentment, we will have been successful.

Another safeguard for the heart is to keep your gaze set heavenward, knowing in another instant we could find ourselves there. As Warren Henderson explains, "Living each day as if the Lord could return at any moment to catch up the Church to heaven (1 Thess. 4:13-18) will safeguard our hearts against discouragement and from settling comfortably into a condemned planet."[6] Contentment will help our spiritual walk and testimony. This attitude is incompatible with the carnal urgings of our flesh, but God provides the strength to those who commit to being content. Resolve to be content in whatever situation the hand of God has put you. In Him, we have everything!

Rose From Brier:

> Thou hast not that, My child, but thou hast Me,
> And am not I alone enough for thee?
> I know it all, know how thy heart was set
> Upon this joy which is not given yet.
>
> And well I know how through the wistful days
> Thou walkest all the dear familiar ways,
> As unregarded as a breath of air,
> But there in love and longing, always there!
>
> I know it all; but from thy brier shall blow
> A rose for others. If it were not so
> I would have told thee. Come then, say to Me:
> My Lord, my Love, I am content with Thee.

— Amy Carmichael[7]

Chapter 14: The Discipline of Thankfulness

And let the peace of God rule in your hearts, to which
also you were called in one body; and be thankful.
(Col. 3:15)

Thankfulness, like contentment, is not dependent upon circumstances. The two characteristics are related, yet distinct. Contentment is being satisfied with what you have; thankfulness is being grateful for what you have. Thankfulness is often verbalized. It contributes to contentment; however, contentment can also lead to thankfulness. There are times when we may not feel content, nonetheless we should still give thanks to God. Usually actions flow from what is in the heart, but sometimes we must simply act in obedience and trust that our heart will be molded by our actions. Have the discipline to lead your heart into thankfulness.

This virtue is highly important. It is a principle in the Old Testament and a command in the New Testament. In the Old Testament, we see over and over again that godly people are grateful people. Also note that giving thanks was considered so important there was a sector of workers in the temple assigned for this sole purpose (Neh. 12:24, 31, 38, 40). In the New Testament, thankfulness is directly commanded: *"Giving thanks **always for all things** to God the Father in the name of our Lord Jesus Christ"* (Eph. 5:20); *"**In everything** give thanks: for this is the will of God in Christ Jesus for you"* (1 Thess. 5:18). And there are many other passages we could turn to, such as Ephesians 5:3-4, Colossians 3:15, 17, and 1 Timothy 2:1. In short, be thankful in everything, for everything, always. To neglect a clear command of God, mind you, is sin.

A Defense Against Sin

Moreover, thankfulness is a spiritual defense, for ingratitude is the impetus for sin. Think about this. Sin results when we say "no" to God's plan, place, and/or principles for us. Lucifer fell when, discontented with his own place in creation, he proudly desired to be like God. Adam and Eve first sinned when they rejected God's command and, also desiring to be like God, ate from the forbidden tree. And down through the ages, the story is the same. Stealing, adultery, homosexuality, idolatry, lying, murder, irreverence, envy, pride: all of these things and more have been done by people who reject living within the commands of God, people who are not satisfied with what they have been given. Indeed, the flesh nature is never gratified; it always wants more: *"All things are full of labor; man cannot express it. The eye is not satisfied with seeing, nor the ear filled with hearing"* (Eccl. 1:8), and *"He who loves silver will not be satisfied with silver; nor he who loves abundance, with increase. This also is vanity"* (Eccl. 5:10). If you surrender to inappropriate lusts, you will only want more and more. Thankfulness is a defense against craving what is outside of God's will.

Thankfulness is in direct opposition to the carnal desires of the flesh; it is a fruit of the Spirit's work in our lives. Satisfaction comes, not in having everything in life, but in having all that matters in life: *"The fear of the Lord leads to life, and he who has it will abide in satisfaction; he will not be visited with evil"* (Prov. 19:23). Accordingly, Elisabeth Elliot states, "Gratitude springs from acceptance of the gifts and the conditions and the circumstances that God gives."[1] It is a deliberate choice to recognize and rejoice in the goodness of God in one's life.

The Blessings of Gratitude

There are so many blessings that accompany a grateful life. Thankfulness can strengthen your faith, awaken you to God's refreshing presence, allow you to profit more from your trials, demonstrate the reality of God to the world around you, help you overcome the devil's devices, and bring glory and pleasure to God. Still, the best praise does not come from those who give thanks because they think they will be blessed for doing so. (Granted, real praise *is* a blessing in itself: *"praise is comely for the upright,"* Ps. 33:1b, KJV).

Neither does the best thanksgiving come from the obligated lips of people who feel this is what Christians "should do" (although thankfulness *is* commanded). Rather, we should aim to praise God from a heart that is motivated and disciplined to be truly thankful!

In this world, we will be disappointed by people, face unfulfilled longings and withered hopes, experience painful circumstances, and have personal failures. Yet, we can and should be thankful *"in all things"* (1 Thess. 5:18) and *"for all things"* (Eph. 5:20). How is this possible? First we must rely on the Lord for the necessary spiritual strength, knowing what God commands, He enables; those He calls, He upholds. We must be committed to thankfulness. Find *something* in your situation for which you can give thanks, or be thankful for how God is using it to develop your character, or even imagine how God *might* use the situation in the future and be thankful for that.

When You Do Not Feel Thankful

After reading Psalm 67:5-7, I was convicted about praising the Lord in all circumstances. He is too great to wait to praise until after the answer comes. God commands us, not to *feel* thankful in every situation, but to give thanks. We do not have to deny our emotions or manufacture positive feelings: in the words of Dr. John G. Mitchel, "To give thanks when you don't feel like it is not hypocrisy; it's obedience."[2] David, the sweet psalmist of Israel, is an example of this. In their book, *31 Days of Praise,* Warren and Ruth Myers point out that David frequently began his psalms by praising the Lord, then continued on to express his troubled emotions, questions, even complaints.

After pouring out his heart before the Lord, David would go on to praise God again, despite the struggles he continued to face.

> [The psalmists] did not deny their feelings or simply ignore them. Nor did they wallow in them until they'd all but drowned. And it doesn't seem that they postponed their praise until they had worked through their emotions and felt better. Instead, they mingled an honest pouring out of their feelings with sincere, God-honoring praise.[3]

Being thankful, regardless of situation or personal feelings, is a path that we should follow. The Myers go on to explain there are blessings for those who do so:

What happens when we follow the example of the psalmists – when we express our impressions and feelings, yet choose to keep praising in spite of how things seem to us? I find that sooner or later (often sooner) the Lord releases me from being a slave to my distressing emotions. He unties the tight knots within me and settles my feelings, though He may not answer my questions about how He's handling my affairs. And when at times praise does not quickly bring inner freedom and joy, I can say, "Lord, I can't praise You in the same way I did last week (or last year). I can't seem to respond to You with the same sense of delight and celebration. But I do choose to lift You high, praising You for what You are and what You mean to me."[4]

At these times, we can, like Paul, be *"sorrowful yet always rejoicing"* (2 Cor. 6:10). It is not a matter of pasting a smile to one's face and making the best of it; rather, we acknowledge our turbulent emotions and troubling circumstances and *praise God anyway*. This is an acceptable sacrifice to God.

Consequently, let us *"Enter into His gates with thanksgiving, and into His courts with praise. Be thankful to Him, and bless His name"* (Ps. 100:4); and, *"Therefore by Him let us continually offer the sacrifice of praise to God, that is, the fruit of our lips, giving thanks to His name"* (Heb. 13:15). It is good for us to give thanks to the Lord (Ps. 33:1, 92:1), and He is worthy of praise (2 Sam. 22:4; Rev. 4:11, 5:12). What an affront it must be to God when we fail to appreciate all He is, all He has done, and all He has given us!

Beyond thankfulness in whatever circumstances we find ourselves, we can always be thankful for our salvation and that God has bestowed us with *"all things that pertain unto life and godliness"* (2 Pet. 1:3), and we should always be thankful for the Person of God Himself (Rom. 1:21). We are thankful for who God is, His attributes, His character, His works. Give thanks to the Lord, for He is our God. He is good, and His mercy endures forever. We thank You, God, for Your Unspeakable Gift! Your works are marvelous! We give thanks at the remembrance of Your holiness. We will sing and praise the Lord among the people of the earth, for generations to come. We are Your people and You are our God – let the world know how awesome You are! Thank you for giving us the victory, for always causing us to triumph in You. Let all people hear of Your marvelous deeds. We will extol and offer thanks to You, the Lord God Almighty – who was, and is, and is to come – for You reign, alone in majesty. You are a wonderful God!

O Lord that lends me life,
Lend me a heart replete with thankfulness!

— Shakespeare[5]

Chapter 15: The Discipline of Faithfulness

Moreover, it is required in stewards that one be found faithful.
(1 Cor. 4:2)

Faith is an inward certainty in unchanging truth, and the word "faithful" refers to character that reflects this confidence; it is an assurance that profoundly affects one's life. Faith is the choice of a disciplined heart; it is not the result of mere feelings. God's own character exemplifies this trait: He is the *faithful* God, Creator, High Priest (Deut. 7:9; 1 Pet. 4:19; Heb. 2:17). He is encompassed by faithfulness and truth and these mark His counsels, works, and judgments.

Accordingly, we can have inward certainty in His unchanging nature in whatever context: salvation, testing, forgiveness, or suffering. As we learned in chapter ten from Oswald Chambers, faith trusts that God is good and does good, though it does not necessarily understand His ways.[1] When we do not know the reason, we can still cling to the Person – because we know that God is good, that He is all-powerful, and that He is unchanging. Paul concisely stated, *"God is faithful"* (1 Cor. 1:9, 10:13); He never changes. Jehovah-jireh provides strength, joy, and peace amid the craziest of circumstances.

Are You Faithful?

Consider how you have seen God's faithfulness in your personal life recently. Jeremiah proclaimed, *"Through the Lord's mercies we are not consumed, because His compassions fail not. They are new every morning; great is Your faithfulness"* (Lam. 3:22-23). His faithfulness, like His compassion, does not fail. On the other hand, David recognized our faithfulness to God was not as enduring, saying, *"the faithful fail from among the children of men"* (Ps. 12:1b, KJV). How would you describe your faithfulness to God? Carl Knot identifies three areas of life which need to be characterized by faithfulness: our love, our stewardship, and our adherence to Scripture. He asks the following probing questions:

Are we faithful in our love for Him or have we left our first love? Many now profess Christ but love the world. Are we faithful stewards (1 Cor. 4:2), or stingy and selfish? Many love materialism and pleasure more than God. Are we faithful to the Word (2 Tim. 2:2) or contemporary so as to please others? Brethren, let us be faithful to God, whatever the cost![2]

The faithful God we serve deserves more faithfulness on the part of His people. He is grieved when we doubt Him and are unfaithful, but delights when we hold to revealed truth. Let it not be said that *"The faithful fail from among the children of men"* while we live and breathe!

The Parable of the Talents

The Parable of the Talents, as recorded in Matthew 25:14-30, includes lessons on faithfulness. In this story, a man was preparing to spend quite some time in a far country. He set his household in order and committed his substance into the hands of his various servants. In his wisdom he gave one five talents, another two, and another one, *"to each according to his particular ability"* (Matt. 25:15, Darby). After he left, the one with five talents worked with what he had to double the amount of money. The one who had been given two also doubled his talents in the same way. However, the servant who had received one talent buried it in the earth.

When the householder returned, the first two servants reported the increase and delivered the ten and four talents, respectively, to him. The master heartily praised each of them with these words: *"Well done, good and faithful servant; you were faithful over a few things, I will make you ruler over many things. Enter into the joy of your lord"* (Matt. 25:21b, 23b). Then the last servant came before the householder. Calling his master harsh and unfair, he bitterly returned the single talent with which he had been entrusted – unchanged. The master responded by addressing him as *"you wicked and lazy servant"* (Matt. 25:26), and rebuked his sloth, explaining that if he did not earn money by working with what had been entrusted to him, at the very least he might have committed the talent to the money-changers (bankers) and returned the talent to the master with interest. In the end, the last servant's lone talent is entrusted to the one who had ten, and the servant himself is thrown out into the darkness.

The first thing to note about this story is that apparently the third servant represents someone who is not saved, as only the lost are ever said to be *"cast...into the outer darkness. There will be weeping and gnashing of teeth"* (Matt. 25:30). Both Christians and unbelievers are the servants of God, though He allows us to choose whether or not we will indeed serve Him; regardless, all are obligated to their Creator. It is interesting that the master in this parable recommended the unfaithful servant commit his talent to the money-changers. As a note of application, if God blesses you with something and you are unable to use it effectively, hand it over to someone who can use and multiply it!

Another thing we can learn from this parable is God gives different "talents" to each of His servants; the word "give" is important – it is not about you or what you can do, but rather what God confers and to what He calls you. Remember, what God commands, He enables; those He calls, He upholds. We are expected to be faithful to what He entrusts us. We are not to compare what we have been afforded to what someone else has received; it is all the Lord's, at any rate! We are to use all our gifts (natural talents, abilities, spiritual gifts); develop these and let them be fruitful; this involves *work*. Where God gives more, He expects more; accordingly, we see that the first two servants in the parable received the same reward for their faithfulness, despite a difference in their ability to serve their master.

This parable in Matthew 25 also lets us see what the true reason for unfaithfulness is. Unfaithful servants do not trust their Lord's character. Like the third servant of the parable, they incorrectly think the Master harsh and unjust, and speak ill of Him. They do not realize the Lord's claim on them: the unfaithful servant grudgingly returned the single talent, grunting, *"There you have what is yours"* (Matt. 25:25) – as if the Master only owns the talent, and not the servant himself and all he has! Recall that *faith* is confidence in the good and unchanging character of God, and that a life that is *faithful* is influenced by this deep-rooted conviction.

Faithful in the Small Things

The test of faithfulness is often found in the "small things": in obscure battles where no (visible) honor is to be gained. Here, discipline accomplishes what good intentions cannot and pushes beyond the point where motivation fails. Consider the words of the Lord:

> *He who is faithful in what is least is faithful also in much; and he who is unjust in what is least is unjust also in much. Therefore if you have not been faithful in the unrighteous mammon, who will commit to your trust the true riches? And if you have not been faithful in what is another man's, who will give you what is your own?* (Luke 16:10-12).

Do you have a faithful heart? Be faithful in the little things; keep busy where you are. Relish the moment, delight in present opportunities, and connect with the people who are in your life now. Do everything you do for the glory of God: *"Therefore, whether you eat or drink, or whatever you do, do all to the glory of God"*; *"and whatever you do, do it heartily, as to the Lord and not to men, knowing that from the Lord you will receive the reward of the inheritance; for you serve the Lord Christ"* (1 Cor. 10:31; Col. 3:23-24). The daily matters of life matter as long as you do everything for the Lord, for His glory. Be careful – your daily activities can dishonor God as easily as they can glorify Him.

It is possible to blaspheme God, not only in our speech, but also in our actions (Rom. 2:24; 1 Tim. 5:14). The prophet Malachi explained how the Jews despised God's name and polluted it through a lack of honor and reverence for God. This was demonstrated by their poor sacrifices, lack of enthusiasm in worship (it was reduced to religious ceremony), and treading down other people. Blasphemy is a disregard for the sacred. As Christians, our entire lives should be sacred; that is, we are to glorify God in our lives. This raises life above mere existence, activities above the daily grind; it is an abundant life, an eternal life that has already begun! May we glorify God in all we do today.

It requires discipline to cultivate this characteristic. The first thing to do is to *"...feed on His faithfulness"* (Ps. 37:3b). Faith is strengthened when we trust God and experience His reliability. Have the stability that comes from the knowledge of God (Hos. 4:1). Be steadfast; don't be rebellious; purpose in your heart to be firm, faithful, trusting God.

Be faithful in the little things. Even activities like flossing one's teeth, moderation in chocolate consumption, and getting up early for some physical and spiritual exercise can be opportunities to develop faithfulness. When you do what you know you should, even though you don't feel like it –it's a good thing! If you aren't disciplined in the little things of life, how will you ever fight the big battles? Exercising discipline builds discipline. If you can't run with the footmen, how shall you contend with horses (Jer. 12:5)? Joe Reese remarks, "Failure in the lesser things of life prophesies utter defeat in the big ones."[3] However, we know that *"those who wait on the Lord shall renew their strength, they shall mount up with wings like eagles, they shall run and not be weary, they shall walk and not faint"* (Isa. 40:31). The Lord gives the strength to continue faithfully.

Faithful in All Things

Faithfulness extends throughout all the many areas of life. You must first be faithful to the Lord; let nothing rob your time, service, or affection for Him. Serve Him well all the days of your life. Also, like Moses (Num. 12:7; Heb. 3:5), you are to be faithful in all your house. When I think about a "house" or "household," I think about relationships. This is certainly an area in which faithfulness is needed. Each relationship should be marked by loyalty, respect, and no tolerance for gossip or slander. An additional application could be made in relation to the House of God, the Church. Be faithful in attendance, faithful in service. Moreover, we are to be faithful, not only among believers, but toward the unsaved as well: the world needs *"faithful ambassadors"* of the kingdom of God (Prov. 13:17).

Be faithful to your word. Do what you say, promptly, even if it turns out to be to your detriment (Ps. 15:4). Do not gossip. Know that you will give an account to God for *"every idle word"* you say (Matt. 12:36). Be steadfast in the unexpected things and in the jobs that end up being harder than anticipated – these are tests of faithfulness! Be conscientious with the talents God has furnished you. Be faithful with your money (Luke 16:10-13). Be responsible with your time. Contrary to the popular colloquialisms of the day, this is not a matter of *having* time, or even *spending* time, and certainly not *killing* time – we *make* time for what is important to us. We complain we do not have the time to be sufficiently devoted to God, yet in reality, we are too lazy to seek God in the time we have. The problem is not one of time, but proper priorities.

All aspects of our life (social activities, work, rest, etc.) should be built around our God. Discipline your life, take control of your habits, and banish laziness (Prov. 13:4; 1 Cor. 9:27). I realize this is neither easy nor comfortable. I am personally convicted of many failings in these areas. But, I do not want to look back on my life and see a series of wasted opportunities and mornings full of snooze buttons (consider Ps. 57:8, 63:1; Mark 1:35). By God's grace, let us be faithful in all things. As a final note, be faithful to invest in those who will be faithful themselves: *"And the things that you have heard from me among many witnesses, commit these to faithful men who will be able to teach others also"* (2 Tim. 2:2). Pray to God for discernment in whom to invest and whom to mentor.

Faithful in the Long Things

In the parable previously discussed, the householder was absent *"a long time"* (Matt. 25:19); it is necessary to be faithful in the "long things." Run the race and finish well. The test of time is a revealing one. Many who ran well have turned aside; be one who finishes well, one who is faithful over the long haul. Persistent faithfulness in the seemingly mundane things of life (e.g. obedience to one's parents or church elders, diligence in completing assigned tasks inside or outside the home, and sharing Christ with others) is a prerequisite for receiving greater opportunities to prove faithfulness. Faithful servants have increased joy and fellowship with the Master. They are well-spoken of, blessed, and rewarded. Note the reward given in the parable is more opportunities for faithfulness, and it is the same for both of the faithful servants. Regardless of the amount of talents they received and delivered to their master, they exhibited the same faithfulness; i.e. they both doubled what was entrusted to them. So it is in the spiritual realm, and so it often is in the realm of men – faithfulness is rewarded with new challenges, new responsibilities, and new opportunities. Faithfulness is not a comfortable thing; it requires a disciplined heart.

The Biblical record is strewn with men and women who were found faithful. For example, when Daniel's enemies tried to find some fault or accusation against him, they were not able to do so *"because he was faithful, nor was there any error or fault found in him"* (Dan. 6:4). Hananiah, brother of Nehemiah, is said to have been *"a faithful man, and feared God more than many"* (Neh. 7:2). What an epithet! Could it, will it, be said of you? Will you be able to look back over a lifetime of faithfulness? Be faithful in the little things (Luke 16:10). Be faithful in all things (1 Tim. 3:11). Be faithful until death (Rev. 2:10). Walk faithfully with the faithful God!

The goal of faithfulness is not that we will do work for God, but that He will be free to do His work through us. God calls us to His service and places tremendous responsibilities on us. He expects no complaining on our part and offers no explanation on His part. God wants to use us as He used His own Son.

— Oswald Chambers[4]

Chapter 16: The Discipline of Joy

Rejoice in the Lord always. Again I will say, Rejoice!
(Phil. 4:4)

In the last chapter we reviewed the Parable of the Talents recorded in Matthew 25; there, we learn faithful servants enter into the joy of their Lord. William MacDonald tells us, "Joy is contentment and satisfaction with God and with His dealings."[1] We serve a joyful God. His joy does not fluctuate as ours is prone to do.

Have you ever wondered what really delights the heart of God? The Bible mentions many things that bring God joy, including: obedience (1 Sam. 15:22), the repentance of the wicked (Ezek. 33:11; Luke 15:7, 10), and His saints (Ps. 149:4). How wonderful to think that God rejoices in His people. In a future day, God will rejoice over restored Israel: *"The Lord your God in your midst, The Mighty One, will save; He will rejoice over you with gladness, He will quiet you with His love, He will rejoice over you with singing"* (Zeph. 3:17). Joy is in the Christian's future as well, as Jude writes: *"Now to Him who is able to keep you from stumbling, and to present you faultless before the presence of His glory with exceeding joy"* (Jude 24). Moreover, the Father has great joy in the Son (Matt. 12:18), who is the source of our joy also. Christ bequeathed His own joy to us (John 15:11, 17:13); the Christian's joy is anchored in the person and promises of God. Since it is founded in the unchanging God of the universe, we need never lose it. Truly, *"...your joy no one will take from you"* (John 16:22b).

While the unregenerate may experience a degree of happiness in life, God is, in fact, the only source of true joy. Those who have not turned to Him seek fulfillment at broken cisterns, but those who come to the wells of salvation find ashes turned to beauty and mourning turned to joy (Isa. 12:3, 61:3; Jer. 2:13). Indeed the saved may well rejoice when thinking of what Christ accomplished at Calvary, as various songwriters have attested: "My joy flows from that grief of

97

Thine; Thy death brings life to me,"[2] and, "The gentle Man of Sorrows is our source of happiness!"[3] An anonymous psalmist, yet on the preceding side of Calvary, called God *"my exceeding joy"* (Ps. 43:4), while David penned these words: *"You will show me the path of life; in Your presence is fullness of joy; at Your right hand are pleasures forevermore"* (Ps. 16:11). Fullness of joy is in God's presence. But is He not present now, here? Are you experiencing fullness of joy?

Restoring Joy

There are certainly times when our joy needs to be restored, as King David prayed, *"Restore to me the joy of Your salvation, and uphold me by Your generous Spirit"* (Ps. 51:12). The context of this passage clarifies the reason David was experiencing a lack of joy; Psalm 51 is his psalm of repentance after his dealings with Bathsheba and her husband Uriah; there is nothing that will kill joy faster than sin. Billy Sunday once said, "If you have no joy, there's a leak in your Christianity somewhere."[4] Consider whether that "leak" may be due to unconfessed sins of omission or commission in your life. Loss of joy is often a telling sign that something is wrong in our relationship with God.

The children of God are not promised that all will be smiles and sunshine; rather, times of sorrow and trouble in the Christian life are assumed, even promised (1 Thess. 3:3-4; 2 Tim. 3:12). But we can know all will be well and the end will be joyful, and in that knowledge we can rejoice even now. Scripture states, *"...weeping may endure for a night, but joy comes in the morning"* (Ps. 30:5b); *"Those who sow in tears shall reap in joy"* (Ps. 126:5). Joy is a calm delight in the promises of God. It is a discipline, and not related to circumstances. Again we see the Christian life is one lived above mere flesh and blood and work and worry – it is a walk upon higher ground with God Himself.

One example of such joy is found in the life of the Old Testament prophet Habakkuk. The overall mood of his book is a rather gloomy prospect of judgment upon the Jews for their sins against God, but see how he ends the opus:

Though the fig tree may not blossom,
Nor fruit be on the vines;

Though the labor of the olive may fail,
And the fields yield no food;
Though the flock may be cut off from the fold,
And there be no herd in the stalls—

Yet I will rejoice in the Lord,
I will joy in the God of my salvation.
The Lord God is my strength;
He will make my feet like deer's feet,
And He will make me walk on my high hills.

To the Chief Musician. With my stringed instruments (Hab. 3:17-19).

Due to rampant idolatry within Israel, God had permitted the Assyrian conquest of the Northern Kingdom; Habakkuk now proclaimed Babylon would decimate Judah for the same reason. Amid widespread wickedness and impending divine chastening, the nation was in desperate straits and life itself hung in a precarious balance. Yet, Habakkuk chose to rejoice in the person of God, His salvation, and the strength He provides. God's joy and strength enabled him to rise above the circumstances around him and even sing praise to the Lord! Enjoy your joy and strength today!

Rejoicing Is a Choice

In the New Testament we find similar examples of rejoicing in dire situations, such as Paul and Silas in Acts 16:16-40. Persecuted for Christ's sake, beaten, and thrown in jail, they proved their joy was not dependent on circumstances. They sang praises and prayed to God in the place they found themselves; *"...and the prisoners were listening to them"* (Acts 16:25) – what a confounding testimony, and who can know its full end? We do not know what fruit might have been born in the lives of these prisoners, nor the full spiritual repercussions from this moment in the lives of Paul and Silas, nor how many Christians down through the ages have been encouraged by this record. We do know that God worked wondrously and people were saved, added to the Church, and joy was multiplied.

Later, Paul the apostle wrote to this gathering of believers in Philippi; the epistle is infused with the words "joy" and "rejoice." Paul let the Philippians know he was still experiencing difficulties, but that he always found something in each situation in which to rejoice (Phil. 1:12-18), resolving, *"...in this I rejoice, yes, and will rejoice"* (v. 18). Warren Henderson comments on this chapter:

> By rejoicing in the Lord always we leave no room for rejoicing in questionable matters or self-centered activities. Once we have learned to rejoice in Christ we learn to turn every situation into a cause of rejoicing, for indeed He is in control of every detail of our lives. Look for something to praise the Lord in. Paul demonstrated this mindset in chapter 1: others were made bold by Paul's bonds, and though some were speaking against Paul the gospel was being preached. The believer must have a yielding spirit (v. 5), then pray about what is causing anxiety, and leave the matter at the throne of grace. Try to find something to praise God about in every situation; rejoicing is a choice![5]

There is always something to rejoice in; fix your mind on that aspect. God does mighty things when His people choose to rejoice in the depths of distress or on the mountains of adversity.

And so it is evident that joy is not dependent upon circumstances; it is a conscious choice that focuses the mind on God's character, works, salvation, and what He is accomplishing in a particular situation. A joyful Christian woman is radiant, sings to God, and delights in His Word. She would rather talk of what the Lord has done than her own circumstances. She forgets self in the joy of serving others. I have been privileged to grow up with an example of such a woman ever before me; my mother's joyful walk with the Lord is a great blessing and encouragement.

The discipline of faithful service brings joy, as long as it is done for Christ and not for people (at some point and on some level, people will always disappoint us), or with anticipated results in mind (expectations for ministry also set up a person for disappointment). The disciplines of contentment and thankfulness are also wonderful tools for building joy. Indeed, "the heights of our joy are measured by the depths of our gratitude," as Ann Voscamp reflects in her book *One Thousand Gifts*.[6] As we are directed to give thanks (Eph. 5:20; 1 Thess. 5:18), we are likewise commanded to rejoice (Ps. 32:11; Phil. 3:1, 4:4). Ann Voscamp continues:

I may feel disappointment and the despair may flood high, but to *give thanks* is an action and *rejoice* is a verb and these are not mere pulsing emotions. While I may not always feel joy, God asks me to give thanks in all things, because He knows that the *feeling* of joy begins in the *action* of thanksgiving.[7]

It takes discipline to keep your heart from being led by circumstances and feelings; you must lead your heart into joy by thanking God for what He has done and by anticipating what He will do – God always keeps His promises.

Joy is a fruit of the Spirit (Gal. 5:22). Remember that as we walk with the Sprit, He produces the fruit in us! Search the Scripture and think about ways to cultivate this fruit:

- Focus on God (Ps. 16:8-11); think of what He does for you, and abide in His presence.
- Rejoice in God's strength and salvation (Ps. 21:1; Isa. 61:10).
- Think of your eternal security (Luke 10:20).
- Keep His Word (Jer. 15:16; Ps. 19:8); obedience to the revealed will of God brings joy (2 Chron. 30:26).
- Seek to win souls, as though bringing in a harvest (Ps. 126:5-6); the Lord's work can be discouraging, but there is joy in the end.
- Rejoice when others exhibit Christlike behavior (Phil. 2:1-4; 3 Jn. 1:4).
- Consider God's provision and protection in life's circumstances (e.g. Est. 8:17; Ps. 5:11).
- Pray (John 16:24; Phil. 1:4).
- Be faithful (Matt. 25:21, 23).
- Relish the moment! Look for divine fingerprints upon your daily life (1 Cor. 10:26; 2 Cor. 2:14).
- Rejoice in trials and persecutions (Luke 6:23; Jas. 1:1-4; 1 Pet. 4:13); keep a heavenly focus; trials produce patience and help perfect character.
- Rejoice when offering sacrifices (1 Chron. 29:9; Neh. 12:43).
- Choose to rejoice (Phil. 4:4). Just do it!

True joy guards the Christian from the cheap but enticing diversions the world has to offer. Matthew Henry tells us, "The joy of the Lord will arm us against the assaults of our spiritual enemies and put our mouths out of taste for those pleasures with which the tempter baits his hooks."[8] In conclusion, then, be encouraged: we can have joy at all times, in all situations, and in every place! Be challenged to give God joy in your own life (via obedience, holiness, quick confession of sin). Be strengthened: *"...the joy of the Lord is your strength"* (Neh. 8:10b).

Scripture for the Troubled Heart:

Hope deferred makes the heart sick, but when the desire comes, it is a tree of life (Prov. 13:12).

He has made everything beautiful in its time. Also He has put eternity in their hearts, except that no one can find out the work that God does from beginning to end (Eccl. 3:11).

He heals the brokenhearted and binds up their wounds (Ps. 147:3).

My flesh and my heart fail; but God is the strength of my heart and my portion forever (Ps. 73:26).

Chapter 17: The Discipline of Patience

Wait on the Lord: be of good courage, and He shall strengthen your heart;
wait, I say, on the Lord.
(Ps. 27:14)

Patience. This is not a particularly agreeable word, unless we are thinking of how it should apply to someone else. Why is this so? We often think of patience as *silent* endurance, but this does not encapsulate the whole idea. There is not room for exasperation or bitterness in biblical patience; rather, it is a spirit of *cheerful* endurance.[1] It is tested in difficult circumstances (persecution or calamity), in waiting, in disruptions, and, as we all know, by difficult people. These situations also provide the best environment to develop and mature patience. Patience is not something we acquire or find one day and then magically nothing bothers us anymore – it is fostered by serenely trusting God in the issues we currently face.

Difficulties, Delays, and Disruptions

Patience involves forbearance and fortitude. It may be showcased in difficult circumstances, whether these are persecutions for the sake of Christ or the trials that accompany life in a world cursed by sin. The latter may be experienced by anyone, while the former are unique to Christians living for Christ. In either case, it is helpful to consider examples of those who have gone before us. Scripture includes the testimonies of many who have suffered for the sake of righteousness, and we would do well to consider them: *"My brethren, take the prophets, who spoke in the name of the Lord, as an example of suffering and patience"* (Jas. 5:10). Other examples may be found in the book of Acts. Suffering persecution patiently is an acceptable sacrifice to God (1 Pet. 2:20).

Job is an example of one who suffered greatly in the trials of life: he lost his wealth, all his children, and his health. Yet many have found comfort in his story, and James the apostle even cited Job's testimony as a positive example in his epistle (Jas. 5:11). Few among us have suffered the bitter sorrows of Job or the cruel persecution waged against the prophets; their examples of forbearance and fortitude should inspire us to be patient in whatever difficult circumstances we do find ourselves.

Patience is "sweet submission to the providential appointment of God."[2] This reminds us God's grace is needed in the delays, interruptions, and disruptions of our lives. Consider Abraham, who waited twenty-five years for his promised son (Gen. 12:1-4, 21:5; Heb. 6:15) and who died without seeing the fulfillment of all the promises he had been given (Heb. 11:8, 39). Yet, he trusted God, worshiped Him, and kept busy while he waited. Elisabeth Elliot has the following to say in reference to waiting:

> Waiting requires patience – a willingness calmly to accept what we have or have not, where we are or where we wish we were, whomever we live or work with. ...A spirit of resistance cannot wait on God. I believe it is this spirit which is the reason for some of our greatest sufferings. Opposing the workings of the Lord in and through our "problems" only exacerbates them. It is *here* and *now* that we must win our victories or suffer defeats. Spiritual victories are won in the quiet acceptance of ordinary events, which are God's "bright servants" standing all around us.[3]

Is there a storm in your life you thought would have passed long ago, or a nagging question you thought should have been answered by this time? Do not faint! Run the race while you're waiting, work while you're waiting, worship while you're waiting. There are lessons to be learned in the waiting, and understanding to be gained in the unanswered questions. Never mistake God's silence for apathy. Sometimes God works through His servants, and sometimes He works in His servants; isn't God more interested in *who* you are than *what* you do? It is no vain thing to wait on the Lord. Elisabeth Elliot remarks: "It is amazing how clear things become when we are *still* before Him, not complaining, not insisting on quick answers, only seeking to hear His word in the stillness, and to see things in His light."[4] God always keeps His promises; hold onto the promises and waiting will not be a heavy weight!

Perhaps you are tried, not by waiting, but by interruptions. To have a plan for the day and see it disrupted, or to have unexpected demands placed upon you, or to have your "me-time" interrupted by a needy individual – this is indeed frustrating. Will you see it as an opportunity to practice patience? And what are these interruptions, but the divine appointments of a sovereign God? The words of Jean Pierre de Caussade on this subject ring true:

> You would be ashamed if you knew what the experiences you call setbacks, upheavals, pointless disturbances, and tedious annoyances really are. You would realize that your complaints against them are nothing more nor less than blasphemies – though this never occurs to you. Nothing happens to you except by the will of God, and yet [God's] beloved children curse it because they do not know it for what it is.[5]

Could it be God has a purpose in the flat tire, the broken leg, or the mere daily business of living: getting together an eatable dinner, correspondence, paying bills, care of teething babies, etc.? Surely He controls all these things. May we delight when our plans are upset by unforeseen circumstances, knowing that God is at work to accomplish His designs. Do not set yourself against these indications of God's ruling hand; allow yourself to be guided through them!

Difficult People

We have examined patience's place in a variety of circumstances: difficult, delayed, and disrupted. Patience is also described as a long-enduring temper, leniency. This makes me think of one's dealings with difficult *people*. Most can point to certain people with whom it seems harder than usual to be patient. The Christian, however, should be patient toward everyone (1 Thess. 5:14).

What a wonderful example we have for this in our Lord! God is patient (Ps. 86:15, 103:8, 145:8; Joel 2:13; Rom. 2:4; 2 Pet. 3:9, 15). Thus, He declared Himself to Moses: *"And the Lord passed before him and proclaimed, 'The Lord, the Lord God, merciful and gracious, longsuffering, and abounding in goodness and truth'"* (Ex. 34:6). He is not only slow to anger, but He is longsuffering (patient) as He continually and gently works in us (e.g. Jas. 1:5; Phil. 1:6). His patience is linked with His mercy, love, and grace. If we are to exhibit patience toward others, we too must be motivated by love (1 Cor. 13:4). Jehovah is, indeed, the God of patience (Rom. 15:5).

Following God's Example

Therefore, it behooves the children of God to demonstrate patience in their own lives (Eph. 4:1-3). It is a characteristic of a servant of the Lord (2 Cor. 6:4; 1 Tim. 6:11; 2 Tim. 2:24-26); we are to be *"...swift to hear, slow to speak, slow to wrath"* (Jas. 1:19b). Patience is a foundation for other Christian graces: *"But let patience have its perfect work, that you may be perfect and complete, lacking nothing"* (Jas. 1:4). The Scripture speaks of patience as essential in the areas of seed-sowing (evangelism, see Luke 8:15), the work of the Lord (Rev. 2:2-3), teaching and exhorting (2 Tim. 4:2), waiting for our blessed hope (Rom. 8:25; 1 Thess. 1:3; Jas. 5:7), and inheriting God's promises (Heb. 6:12). Hudson Taylor, missionary to China, remarked, "There are three indispensable requirements for a missionary: 1. Patience, 2. Patience, 3. Patience."[6] Anyone who serves the Lord, whether at home or abroad, can agree that patience is needed!

Considering the examples set for us by Abraham, Job, the prophets, the early Christians, and, foremost of all, the Lord Jesus – endure: *"Therefore we also, since we are surrounded by so great a cloud of witnesses, let us lay aside every weight, and the sin which so easily ensnares us, and let us run with endurance* [patience] *the race that is set before us"* (Heb. 12:1). Patience is a fruit of the Spirit (Gal. 5:22), but it is generally grown in unpleasant circumstances (Rom. 5:3; Jas. 1:2-4), or from contact with relatively unpleasant people. Do not waste a good problem! Pray you learn all God would have you learn from a situation.

Perhaps you, like I, feel inadequate? It may well have been said of me: *"For ye have need of patience, that, after ye have done the will of God, ye might receive the promise"* (Heb. 10:36, KJV). This passage tells us to endure, to keep doing what we should be doing. Know that you can be strengthened with all mightiness according to the glorious dynamic power of God so that you, too, can long-suffer with joyfulness (Col. 1:11)!

In conclusion, be encouraged: God is great in His patience; He postpones judgment on the wicked, and works with His children in order to bring them into conformity with His Son. He does not upbraid us when we fall short. Be challenged: it takes spiritual strength to rule one's spirit, to not "fly off the handle" or "snap" at problems (especially people problems). Patience demonstrates love, discretion, meekness, and wisdom.

God's children should be characterized by patience in all things to all people. Patience is rewarded in the end. Use the circumstances and people in your life to develop longsuffering! Endure patiently without complaint. Be at peace; expressing impatience or saying you are stressed out is the same as saying that God is not ruling your life well and so you have to worry about it. Having an attitude of patience will affect your speech and actions toward others. Be lowly and meek, remembering God's patience toward you. Paul charged Timothy, *"You therefore must endure hardship as a good soldier of Jesus Christ"* (2 Tim. 2:3). This is not our final resting place, but we press on in patience. Keep on keeping on. Rule your spirit; discipline your heart.

Warren Wiersbe has the following remarks on patience:

- Life's trials are not easy. But in God's will, each has a purpose. Often He uses them to enlarge you.
- Those times when you feel like quitting can be times of great opportunity, for God uses your troubles to help you grow.
- Some of your greatest blessings come with patience.[7]

Chapter 18: The Discipline of Submission

Therefore He says: "God resists the proud, but gives
grace to the humble." Therefore submit to God.
(Jas. 4:6b-7a)

Submit. Isn't it odd how the flesh instantly rears up against that word? Why ever would we be talking about "the discipline of submission" in this modern age of enlightened, empowered, entitled individuals? At best, isn't this a rather backward way of thinking? Submission is so ill-thought of in modern society that we have largely forgotten what it truly means. It is different from *accede*, which is to agree. Neither is it the same as *concede*, which means to comply, but does not address one's attitude. The Greek word translated "submit" in the New Testament is *hupotasso*, a combination of the words "arrange" and "under."[1] In a previous chapter, we learned discipline is to put oneself under orders; submission is akin to this, and is to put one's will under another's. There is nothing wrong with having a will, naturally, but we are responsible for what we do with it. Obedience can be forced, but submission is a matter of the heart.

Let us pause and consider our position in this universe. We are created by and cared for by God. Augustine wrote, "Thou hast created us for Thyself, and our hearts are restless until they rest in Thee."[2] God brought about our existence and sustains it from day to day. We are, therefore, dependent creatures. Dependence necessitates obedience, which, in turn, is the foundation of discipline. As mentioned previously, to be disciplined is to put oneself under orders. God calls us to walk in a certain way, and it is when we obey His call that we find fulfillment, joy, and blessing, for it is then that we are who we were created to be.

We are to submit, first and foremost, to God. James wrote: *"...Therefore He says: 'God resists the proud, but gives grace to the humble.' Therefore submit to God..."* (Jas. 4:6b-7a). Those who come to God must do so on His terms. Submission is necessary for salvation (Rom. 10:3) and leads to life (Heb. 12:9). In truth, all are subject to God (1 Cor. 15:27-28; Eph. 1:22, 5:24; Phil. 3:21; Heb. 2:8; 1 Pet. 3:22). He is great in power, mighty in mercy, strong in love – is it not easy to submit to such a Commander as this?

Learning to Surrender

If submission is arranging one's will underneath another's will, it is very much like surrender. Surrender can be voluntary. It can also be obligatory in the face of overpowering strength. One day, all – even those who have made themselves His enemies – will submit themselves under the great power of God (Ps. 66:3); all will bow before the Lord Jesus Christ, if not as their Savior, then as their Judge (Phil. 2:10-11). But presently it is the action of God's children to submit to the good, acceptable, and perfect will of God (Rom. 12:2). We may not understand it; we may not see what God is working out of a particular circumstance, but the truth of Romans 12:2 remains. The will of God is good. The will of God is acceptable. The will of God is perfect. The word "acceptance" makes me think of gifts presented and received. We accept God's will when we receive as a gift all He hands us. Unconditional surrender is total acceptance: a life lived in wild abandon to God. Submission. Surrender. Sacrifice: these characterize real Christianity.

And yet, we must rethink the term "sacrifice." C. T. Studd, a wealthy British athlete who in the late nineteenth century left fame and fortune to pioneer missionary work in China, India, and Africa, recognized this: "If Jesus Christ be God and died for me, then no sacrifice can be too great for me to make for Him."[3] David Livingstone, missionary to and explorer of Africa, experienced ill health, the death of his wife and three of his children, and prolonged absence from his remaining family; this is what he told students at Cambridge about leaving the "benefits" of England:

> For my own part, I have never ceased to rejoice that God has appointed me to such an office. People talk of the sacrifice I have made in spending so much of my life in Africa. . . . Is that a sacrifice which brings its own blest reward in healthful activity, the consciousness of doing good, peace of mind, and a bright hope of a

glorious destiny hereafter? Away with the word in such a view, and with such a thought! **It is emphatically no sacrifice. Say rather it is a privilege**. Anxiety, sickness, suffering, or danger, now and then, with a foregoing of the common conveniences and charities of this life, may make us pause, and cause the spirit to waver, and the soul to sink; but let this only be for a moment. All these are nothing when compared with the glory which shall be revealed in and for us. **I never made a sacrifice**.[4] (emphasis added)

There are others who would agree with C. T. Studd and Dr. Livingston:

Any sacrifices we make are no sacrifices at all, when seen in the light of Calvary. Besides all this, we only give to the Lord what we cannot keep anyway and what we have ceased to love.

— William MacDonald[5]

He is no fool who gives what he cannot keep to gain that which he cannot lose.

— Jim Elliot[6]

Come as the fire, and purge our hearts with sacrificial flame;
Let our whole soul an offering be to our Redeemer's name.

— Andrew Reed[7]

We are surrounded by a great cloud of witnesses; the way of the cross is the way of submission. What areas of your heart need more of this discipline? We surrender something to accept something: this life is both a letting go and a laying hold, a dying and a resurrecting. What is God calling you to surrender, or to accept?

Learning Submission Through Authority

Not only are we to submit to God, but we are also to submit to the authorities that come from God. We need no reason for this other than God commands it, as we have already come to see that we owe Him unquestioning allegiance. But if some would inquire whether God really thinks our submission to others is a "big deal," let them know that if they take themselves out from underneath the God-appointed authorities in their lives, it is nothing short of rebellion against God

Himself. At that point, they are not doing the will of God, but of the devil. They have not escaped authority, but rather have put themselves under satanic authority, and that cannot end well. Compliance to the human authorities in our lives is indeed important; God is, in fact, using these structures to teach us submission to Him.

God includes instructions for who is to submit to whom in various interpersonal areas where human wills may collide: children are to obey and honor their parents (Eph. 6:1-3), wives are to submit to their own husbands (Eph. 5:22, 24; Col. 3:18; Titus 2:5; 1 Pet. 3:1, 5), servants to their masters (Titus 2:9; 1 Pet. 2:18 – consider the application to employee/employer relationships), citizens to their governments (Rom. 13:1-5; Titus 3:1; 1 Pet. 2:13). Within the realm of church order, Christians are to submit to local church leadership (Heb. 13:17); also, women are to defer the leadership of the local church and the verbal ministry of those meetings to the men (1 Cor. 14:34; Tit. 1:5-6).

Further instruction on the differing ministries of men and women within the church is provided in 1 Corinthians 11, where it is prefaced by the following statement: *"But I want you to know that the head of every man is Christ, the head of the woman is man, and the head of Christ is God"* (v. 3). Christ, the Son of God, is equal with God the Father, and recognizes the Father as His Head in divine order. Just because things are equal in *value* (see Gal. 3:28) does not mean they are to occupy the same *position*. The woman is equal to the man in value; yet, she is to recognize man as her head, according to the order God has set in place. Some find this difficult; perhaps this is why God commanded a visible, symbolic reminder of His glory as it relates to His authority later on in 1 Corinthians 11. Usually the people who long for a different role or ministry are the same people who are not fulfilling the role and/or ministries with which they have been divinely entrusted. But if you are not faithful with what you have, you will never be faithful to what you do not have, for you are seeking your will and not God's. Approaching service from such a vantage point will end in disaster.

Submitting to Each Other

As we continue to ponder exhortations to submission, we see we are also to put our will under that of all other Christians in general: *"Submitting to one another in the fear of God"* (Eph. 5:21); *"Likewise you younger people, submit yourselves to your elders. Yes, all of you be submissive to one another, and be clothed with humility, for 'God resists the proud, but gives grace to the humble'"* (1 Pet. 5:5). This indicates we can "practice" the discipline of submission in all our interactions! Are you willing to sacrifice for members of the body of Christ? Will you forfeit your plans, your preferences, even your "rights," if need be? Christ held His rights with a loose hand indeed. But certainly there are individuals to whom it is harder to yield? Remember that how you treat the lowliest believer in Christ is a reflection on how you treat the Lord Himself (Matt. 25:40).

Be a submissive, obedient person (this is the will of God for everyone). There is no fancy three-point outline for accomplishing this: it is simply done. As the old Nike slogan states, "Just do it!" When it comes to the clear will of God, we do not have to wait to "feel led"; if the Lord has spoken, it does not matter how we feel. (This is in opposition to the common worldview that says everyone decides what is right for themselves.)

"Love's Strength Stands in Love's Sacrifice"

A 19th-century monk named Ugo Bassi saw submission and acceptance symbolized in a vineyard. He regularly preached in a hospital in Rome; one sermon on John 15 was later recorded in poetic form by Harriet E. H. King. It tells us the life of the vine is "not of pleasure nor of ease." It ekes out a hard existence staked to a hillside, pouring its efforts into its grapes, which are then torn away and smashed in the winepress, while the vine itself is pruned back until it is "despoiled, disfigured, left a leafless stock, alone through all the dark days that shall come." Yet, the wine it produced gladdens the heart of man. The land is full of joy, but who takes thought of the vine? But though it gives happiness to others, it is "not bitter for the torment undergone, not barren for the fullness yielded up." The vine finds itself seemingly forsaken, and yet this is its motto:

> Measure thy life by loss instead of gain;
> Not by the wine drunk but by the wine poured forth;
> For love's strength standeth in love's sacrifice,
> And whoso suffers most hath most to give.[8]

As branches of the All-Giving Vine, it is our calling to abide in Him and bear fruit, not for ourselves, but for the glory of God. This is love and joy (John 15:1-13).

Submission. Surrender. Sacrifice. These are the marks of real Christianity, for they are marks of Christ. God the Son is ever in submission to God the Father. This was never seen more clearly than at Calvary: *"Though He was a Son, yet He learned obedience [hupakoe,* by implication, submission] *by the things which He suffered"* (Heb. 5:8). He surrendered His position in heaven, His time, His work, His life, Himself: *"Who Himself bore our sins in His own body on the tree, that we, having died to sins, might live for righteousness – by whose stripes you were healed"* (1 Pet. 2:24). Christ surrendered so much; what is it that you are withholding from Him? Or are you submitted, accepting where He has you, what He has given you, and what He would have you do? This requires discipline, but total submission to the Right Person (and those He indicates you are also to submit to) is the path of peace and blessing. Do you have a submitted heart?

Perfect submission, all is at rest;
I and my Savior are happy and blest!
Watching and waiting, looking above,
Filled with His goodness, lost in His love.

— Fanny J. Crosby[9]

Chapter 19: The Discipline of Prayer

"We are too busy to pray, and so we are too busy to have power.
We have a great deal of activity, but we accomplish little; many
services but few conversions; much machinery but few results."
(R.A. Torrey)[1]

Prayer is, quite possibly, the weakest area of my spiritual life. I find
I echo the disciples' plea as my own: *"...Lord, teach us* [me] *to
pray..."* (Luke 11:1). It would be helpful to examine each part of this
request. First, we see it is to the *Lord* we must turn. In his helpful book,
Lord, Teach Us to Pray, Andrew Murray writes, "Moses gave neither
command nor regulation with regard to prayer; even the prophets say
little directly of the duty of prayer; it is Christ who teaches to pray."[2]
And such a teacher we have! Christ knows prayer, as the record of the
gospels declares (e.g. Matt. 14:23, 19:13, 26:36-45; Mark 1:35, 6:46;
Luke 3:21, 5:16, 6:12, 9:18, 28-29, 11:1, 22:41-46; John 17). He also
has the patience and gentleness necessary to instruct such rough pupils
as we present ourselves, and He has access to the believer's heart
through the indwelling Spirit of God.

Learning to Pray

The disciples requested the Lord *teach* them to pray, and we also
find ourselves in need of instruction. In his booklet, *Lord, Teach Us to
Pray*, Andrew Murray comments, "At first there is no work appears so
simple; later on, none that is more difficult; and the confession is forced
from us: We know not how to pray as we ought."[3] He also makes the
following observation: "Jesus never taught His disciples how to preach,
only how to pray."[4] Although prayer is a worthy subject for a topical
Bible study, and we can learn much from the prayers recorded in
Scripture, this alone will not revitalize one's prayer life. Prayer is
learned, not in the classroom, but in the closet. Christ teaches us when
we come to Him privately on our knees.

Returning to the disciples' request in Luke 11:1, please note the use of the word *us*. What we learn from this is that we need to make a personal acknowledgement of failure and plea for grace in this area. Finally, we come to what it was the disciples wanted to know: *to pray.* Someone has said, "Nothing lies beyond the reach of prayer except that which lies outside of the will of God."[5] Andrew Murray states, "Though in its beginnings prayer is so simple that the feeble child can pray, yet it is at the same time the highest and holiest work to which man can rise."[6] Prayer reminds us how much we need the Lord; it is an opportunity to praise, worship, and thank Him; it realigns our priorities; it reminds us of what we have in common with other saints; it is a spiritual weapon (Eph. 6:13, 18-20).

Christ responded to the request of His disciples with the words of what has often been called "The Lord's Prayer" and, less frequently but perhaps more correctly, "The Disciples' Prayer." That this was not a prayer made by the Lord is evident by the inclusion of a request for forgiveness; Christ never needed forgiveness of sins. Instead, He offered this as a model to the disciples, saying *"...when you pray, say..."* (Luke 11:2). The context of Scripture as a whole ensures this was intended as a guideline, not as a subject for *"vain repetitions"* (Matt. 6:7). Clearly, our prayers should not be a replication of this exact appeal.

The prayer begins with worship and regard for God's interests. Physical needs and forgiveness of sin are then addressed. A similar passage of Scripture in Matthew 6 suggests it is appropriate to end prayer on a note of praise or worship. Incidentally, it appears from Matthew 6 that Christ had already provided His disciples with instruction on prayer near the beginning of His public ministry. It was toward the end of His ministry that His disciples came to Him with the request in Luke 11. The Lord repeated the same teaching presented earlier (see Matthew 6-7), with an added parable highlighting the importance of persistence in prayer. This can be an encouragement for those of us who do not feel adequate in prayer, even after being taught on the subject. It is a joy to keep coming back to Him who gives wisdom to the foolish without reproaching them (Jas. 1:5)!

The example prayer in Luke 11 begins, *"...Our Father in heaven, hallowed be Your name. Your kingdom come. Your will be done on earth as it is in heaven"* (v. 2). The prayer is addressed to God the

Father and starts off by expressing reverence for God's person and deference to His interests. From the story of the woman at the well told in John 4, we learn, as Andrew Murray expresses it, "The Father *seeks* worshippers: our worship satisfies His loving heart and is a joy to Him. He seeks *true worshippers*, but finds many not such as He would have them. True worship is that which is *in spirit and truth*."[7] Worship, to be acceptable to the Eternal God, must be Spirit-led and according to His truth – we must approach Him His way. Christ told the woman at the well that in a coming day worship would not be restricted to a certain location, Jerusalem. Andrew Murray continues with the following observation:

> As God is Spirit, not bound by space or time, but in His infinite perfection always and everywhere the same, so His worship would henceforth no longer be confined by place or form, but spiritual as God Himself is spiritual. A lesson of deep importance. How much our Christianity suffers from this, that it is confined to certain times and places. A man who seeks to pray earnestly in the church or in the closet, spends the greater part of the week or the day in a spirit entirely at variance with that in which he prayed. His worship was the work of a fixed place or hour, not of his whole being. God is a spirit: He is the Everlasting and Unchangeable One; what He is, He is always and in truth. Our worship must even so be in spirit and truth: His worship must be the spirit of our life; our life must be worship in spirit as God is Spirit.[8]

In the Old Testament, God promised to hear the prayers made in the temple (1 Kgs. 8:28-53; 2 Chron. 6:20-42), which was even called *"the House of Prayer"* (e.g. Luke 19:46). In the current era, Christians are the temple of God (1 Cor. 3:16, 6:19; Eph. 2:19-22), and we are called to live a life of worship and of prayer, and worship must be at the forefront of our prayers.

The prayer recorded in Luke 11 moves on to address physical needs. Note the *daily bread* requested is an actual, present need; these are matters to lay before the throne of grace. In contrast, many of the things I pray for are more like "daily wants."

The next thing requested is forgiveness of sins: "As bread is the first need of the body, so forgiveness for the soul."[9] Keep short accounts with God. Do not allow unconfessed sin to hinder your fellowship with Him or your ministry for Him. Finally, it is good to end prayer with praise for what God has done or worship for who He is. No matter what it is that has driven us to prayer, as we gaze upward we are refreshed in His presence, "and the things of earth will grow strangely dim, in the light of that glorious grace."[10] There is always cause to praise and worship our God!

Hindrances to Prayer

Let us now consider what might keep a person from prayer. Some wonder why they should pray if God is sovereign over the universe – won't what He wants to happen take place apart from our asking? Regardless, we are repeatedly commanded to pray (Rom. 12:12; Eph. 6:18; Phil. 4:6; Col 4:2; 1 Thess. 5:17; 1 Tim. 2:1-2). Also, as previously mentioned, we see the example of Jesus Christ in prayer; do we not want to follow His example in all things? Moreover, James tells us the fervent prayer of the righteous, aligned with the will of God, has much power (Jas. 5:16b-18) and that we lack because we fail to ask, or we ask with the wrong reasons (Jas. 4:2-3). This should be more than enough to convince us of the importance God places on prayer.

Elisabeth Elliot provides the following observation on prayer:

> It is a law of the universe. God ordained that certain physical laws should govern the operation of this world. Books simply will not stay put on a table without the operation of the law of gravity. There are spiritual laws as well. Certain things will not happen without the operation of prayer. God could cause books to stay on tables by what theologians call "divine *fiat*." Everything we pray for could occur in the same way, but that is not how things were arranged. Pascal, the great French thinker, said that in prayer God gives us "the dignity of causality."[11]

God chooses to operate through the prayers of His people, and so prayer works. Therefore, thoughts of His sovereignty should spur us on, not deter us, from prayer. Neither should our own inadequacy prevent us from confidently approaching God in prayer, as Andrew Murray offers this encouragement:

> They are discouraged and kept from prayer by the thought that they cannot come to the Father as they ought or as they wish. Child of

God! Listen to your Teacher. He tells you that when you go to private prayer your first thought must be: The Father is in secret, the Father waits me there. Just because your heart is cold and prayerless, get you into the presence of the loving Father. As a father pitieth his children, so the Lord pitieth you. Do not be thinking of how little you have to bring God, but of how much He wants to give you. Just place yourself before, and look up into, His face; think of His love, His wonderful, tender, pitying love. Just tell Him how sinful and cold and dark all is: it is the Father's loving heart will give light and warmth to yours. …Not on the wrong or the fervent feeling with which I pray does the blessing of the closet depend, but upon the love and the power of the Father to whom I there entrust my needs.[12]

However frail our prayers may be, it is far worse to offer none at all. The value of our prayers does not end with us; the Holy Spirit Himself makes intercession for us (Rom. 8:26), and we come, not on our own merits, but in the name of Jesus Christ the Lord (John 14:13-14, 15:16, 16:23-26).

As Amy Carmichael, missionary to India, meditated on the *conflict* Paul stated he had for the Colossians (Col. 2:1), she took this to refer to the conflict of prayer, for indeed prayer *is* conflict. She wrote the following to her "family" at Dohnavur about the struggles she personally faced – what discouraged her from praying, and what encouraged her to continue the spiritual conflict; may it encourage us on as well:

With what did I struggle?
1. With all that says to me, what is the use of your praying? So many others, who know more of prayer than you do, are praying. What difference does it make whether you pray or not? Are you sure that your Lord is listening? Of course He is listening to the other prayers but yours are of such small account, are you really sure He is "bending His ear" to *you*?
2. With all that suggests that we are asked to give too much time to prayer. There is so much to do. Why set aside so much time to pray?
3. With all that discouraged me personally – perhaps the remembrance of past sin, perhaps spiritual or physical tiredness; with anything and everything that keeps me back from what occupied St. Paul so often – vital prayer.

What will help me most in this wrestle?

1. The certain knowledge that our insignificance does not matter at all, for we do not come to the Father in our own name but in the Name of His beloved Son. His ear is always open to that Name. Of this we can be certain.

2. The certain knowledge that this is Satan's lie; he is much more afraid of our prayer than our work. (This is proved by the immense difficulties we always find when we set ourselves to pray. They are much greater than those we meet when we set ourselves to work.)

3. Isaiah 44:22 and kindred words, with 1 John 1:9, meet all distress about sin. Isaiah 40:29-31 with 2 Corinthians 12:9, 10 meets everything that spiritual or physical weariness can do to hinder. Psalm 27:8 with Isaiah 45:19 meets all other difficulties. And the moment we say to our God, "Thy face, Lord, will I seek," His mighty energies come to the rescue. (See Colossians 1:2, 9) *Greater, far greater, is He that is in us than he that is against us. Count on the greatness of God.*[13]

Our prayers matter. They are offered in the name of Jesus Christ, the Lord. They are a powerful weapon against the enemy. They are empowered by the strength of God.

Don't Neglect Your Prayer Life!

When did prayer become neglected? When did the prayer meeting become an optional gathering of the church? Was it around the time we ceased to see the wide-sweeping movement of the Spirit of God? To excuse themselves from this vital church meeting, people cite a variety of reasons such as: health and work (these may be valid necessities), sports and other activities that may approach idolatry, and young children or other family members (reminding us of the man who would not come to the banquet because he had married a wife, when indeed, what is a better place for a family to be gathered than with the saints in prayer!). Then again, there is perhaps the lamest excuse of all – a need for "personal" time or relaxation. Is this discipline? Is this really what our priorities look like?

No man is greater than his prayer life. ... We have many organizers, but few agonizers; many players and payers, few pray-ers; many singers, few clingers; lots of pastors, few wrestlers; many fears, few tears; much fashion, little passion; many interferers, few intercessors; many writers, but few fighters. Failing here, we fail everywhere.

— Leonard Ravenhill[14]

Furthermore, when we do assemble to pray, what is it that we are requesting of God? Mike Attwood has this observation: "I listen to the prayers, and it's all about sick people getting better, keeping the saints out of heaven, that seems to be our chief objective!"[15] It is true that we often seem more concerned about our own physical health than the one hundred seven souls entering eternity each minute, most without Christ.[16] Do we pray for Christian coworkers? For the growth and edification of the saints? For revival? For salvation of souls? For a mighty work of God?

> Thou art coming to a King,
> Large petitions with thee bring;
> For His grace and power are such
> None can ever ask too much.

— John Newton[17]

It is an interesting study to examine the prayers recorded in the Bible. How widely these differ from my usual prayers! Paul, for example, seems to have had a long prayer list that included the churches in Rome, Corinth, Ephesus, Philippi, Colossi, Thessalonica, as well as individuals such as Timothy and Philemon. The following is an example of one of his prayers for the church at Ephesus:

For this reason I bow my knees to the Father of our Lord Jesus Christ, from whom the whole family in heaven and earth is named, that He would grant you, according to the riches of His glory, to be strengthened with might through His Spirit in the inner man, that Christ may dwell in your hearts through faith; that you, being rooted and grounded in love, may be able to comprehend with all the saints what is the width and length and depth and height— to know the love of Christ which passes knowledge; that you may be filled with all the fullness of God. Now to Him who is able to do exceedingly abundantly above all that we ask or think, according to the power that works in us, to Him be glory in the Church by Christ Jesus to all generations, forever and ever. Amen (Eph. 3:14-21).

Perhaps our own prayer lives would be rejuvenated if we made a study of the prayers in Scripture, and offered similar appeals. We might seize these as a model, just as the disciples received a model prayer from the Lord. We know we are to pray according to the will of God, so it seems appropriate to pray according to His will as revealed in His Word (1 Jn. 5:14).

Paul, recognizing the importance of prayer and the benefits for those who pray as well as those prayed for, had no qualms about requesting prayer for himself: *"Now I beg you, brethren, through the Lord Jesus Christ, and through the love of the Spirit, that you strive together with me in prayers to God for me"* (Rom. 15:30). Prayer is a splendid means of co-laboring with other Christians. Have you invested in the ministry of the brother who will speak from God's Word this Sunday, of the sister who has an after-school Bible club on Monday, of the student who is actively sharing the gospel with classmates throughout the week, or of the missionary who serves abroad?

Be in prayer: for church elders, for blessings, for problems (Heb. 13:7; Jas. 5:16b-18). Brian Gunning remarks on the importance of praying for the church: "The discipline of prayer indicates whether we are interested in solutions to assembly problems, or just interested in talking about them. ...It [prayer] is the only solution. It works because God chooses to work by it."[18] It is true we are much more prone to gossip about problems than talk *to God* about them; this should never be! Public prayer is the fruit of private prayer. Are we a praying people?

Paul exhorted the Colossians, *"Continue earnestly in prayer, being vigilant in it with thanksgiving"* (Col. 4:2). Never resist the urge to pray. We know *"...the effectual fervent prayer of a righteous man availeth much"* (Jas. 5:16b, KJV). It is important to come before the Lord in righteousness, as the psalmist states, *"If I regard iniquity in my heart, the Lord will not hear me"* (Ps. 66:18, KJV; see also Prov. 15:8, 29, 28:9). May our prayers be fervent, and by God's grace may they be effectual. *"Lord, teach us to pray."*

I am so busy now that if I did not spend two or three hours each day in prayer, I would not get through the day.
— Martin Luther[19]

Chapter 20: The Discipline of Purity

Flee also youthful lusts; but pursue righteousness, faith, love,
peace with those who call on the Lord out of a pure heart.
(2 Tim. 2:22)

In chapter twelve we looked at the topic of self-control, including a brief look at the discipline of emotions. We found this is not only possible, but necessary for a serious disciple of Christ. While we cannot necessarily help what feelings may arise in our hearts, we are responsible for what we do with those feelings. We want to bring our emotions captive to the knowledge of Christ, that is, into accordance with His teachings. We specifically examined the emotions of anger and anxiety. In this chapter, I would like to revisit this topic by examining the discipline of purity in general, then specifically looking at emotional promiscuity, which I think is fairly prevalent among young Christian women who otherwise seem to have high standards of purity. This is a long chapter, but I believe the length is merited by the importance of the topic.

God's Gifts

While each Christian must learn the discipline of purity, this chapter is written chiefly to those who are not married. Therefore, before discussing this discipline, it would be good to review what the Bible has to say about singleness. We know that marriage is ordained by God, and in 1 Corinthians 7 we read He gives grace for those called to singleness. The word for gift is *charisma*, and it comes from the root word *charis*, which means grace.[1] God in His grace gives us wonderful gifts. The gifts we receive, from friends and family or from God, are not necessarily the things we would have chosen for ourselves. However, we can always count on God to confer good gifts, even if we don't always understand His ways.

God offers the gift of salvation from sin and eternal life through Jesus Christ (Rom. 5:15, 6:23). The Holy Spirit Himself is a pledge from God received upon salvation (Acts 10:45). A variety of "spiritual gifts" are referenced for us in Romans 12, 1 Corinthians 12, and Ephesians 4. Moreover, God provides grace for the particular ministry to which He calls a person (Eph. 3:7). He has already granted us everything we need to please Him; He has graciously *"blessed us with every spiritual blessing in the heavenly places in Christ"* (Eph. 1:3). If we can trust Him with these eternal matters (e.g. salvation), can we not trust Him with such temporal matters as marriage and singleness?

We are to receive all God's gifts with an attitude of gratitude, not as spoiled toddlers who burst into tantrums if they don't get their own way, or who see someone else with the gift they wanted and try to grab it for themselves! Moreover, we are to use the gifts of God for their intended purpose, which is to fulfill our calling in Christ.

We know each gift God furnishes is good (Jas. 1:17) and that He will not withhold from us anything that would be good for us to have (Ps. 84:11). The gifts God grants you, whether spiritual gifts as in the context of Ephesians 4:12-13 to edify the church, or gifts of grace to remain permanently single or to sustain you in the interim prior to marriage, are for the glory of God! Therefore, *"As each one has received a gift, minister it to one another, as good stewards of the manifold grace of God"* (1 Pet. 4:10). Do not let yourself become the measure and boundary of your world – open your eyes to the greater good God is working in and through you!

Our Longings

An understanding of God's gifts allows us to see that a godly woman is not necessarily single because the right man has not come around or because she lacks feminine charm but because, at least for the present, God wants her to be single and provides grace for her to remain single. I think young people often get too worked up trying to determine whether or not they are called to singleness. It's really not too difficult: if you are not married, then, at least for the present, you are called to be single and He will sustain you while you are single! That is, you are in the situation God has for you at this time. Possibly later you may experience marriage. But be content, whatever state you are in; do not strive for a gift, calling, or talent with which God has not entrusted you (1 Cor. 7:20).

Carolyn McCulley points out, "It's not wrong to desire marriage or to ask God for it. The problem is when we do not humbly and peaceably accept God's will for our lives *right now*."[2] John Calvin wrote, "The evil in our desire typically does not lie in what we want, but that we want it too much."[3] Longings are not wrong. Sometimes God gives us longings and then fulfills them so we may rejoice at His provision. Sometimes God gives us longings and leaves them unfulfilled so we may come to further recognize our need for Him.

Aside from the purposes just mentioned, Scripture indicates two other possible reasons for unfulfilled desires. First, in James 4:2-3 we read of Christians whose desires were not granted because they either did not pray about them or because their prayer requests were proffered with bad motives (to cater to their flesh nature). Second, in Ezekiel 24:16 we read how this prophet's wife died; Ezekiel's *"desire"* was taken away to further God's will and his own ministry (i.e. her death would be used as an object lesson to warn the Jewish nation of the coming slaughter and captivity). If our desires be not granted, may it be to further God's ministry and not because we are in the flesh!

Complete satisfaction cannot be found in any human relationship or situation – this is found only in the Lord. As God's child, trust Him with your longings; as God's bondservant, surrender to Him any expectations of physical or emotional security. Be committed to fostering your relationship with the Lord and to serving Him with the time, resources, and energy allotted to you as a single woman. Singleness is not an intermission in life; life does not begin at marriage. The life of a godly woman, single or otherwise, ought to be a continuum of service for God and for the Church body as a whole. It would be strange if a heart only pumped blood for the liver. So also the single woman should not allow her time or consideration to be monopolized by the "available" men within the body of Christ. Be committed to serving all: young, old, single, families, children, etc. If you are still totally stymied and feeling marginalized, look for the lonely people (they are everywhere), and seek to be a blessing to them.

Loneliness is real, but the loneliness of a single woman busy investing in the lives of others is far different than the loneliness of a single woman who pushes people away to engage in self-pity.

Incidentally, John Piper calls self-pity "the response of pride to suffering,"[4] and is that ever true! Consider that your future husband (if God calls you to marry) would be glad to know you are single right now; God can bring you to the right man's attention in His divine way and time. Turn your solitude into prayer, your loneliness into service, your emptiness into love for God and others. In the words of Edith Stein, who was murdered in Auschwitz, "Fill up the emptiness of your heart with love for God and your neighbor."[5] In this way, those who pass through the Valley of Baca (lit. "weeping") make it a well, a spring to refresh themselves and others (Ps. 84:6).

Physical Purity

Of course, purity is not a topic for single women only. Being married does not lead to personal fulfillment, security, the satisfaction of every longing, or freedom from struggling with sinful lusts. What, then, should be the approach of a Christian woman towards this topic of purity? I believe it begins with honesty.

The gospel lets us be honest before God. It lets us acknowledge that we are sinners, that we are a mess. After we receive God's gift of salvation, He chooses not to remove us from the struggle with sin, but to equip us in this battle. Grace steps in, and each can say: God loves and accepts me in the place I am here and now; however, He loves me too much to leave me here, and will continue to work in me and perfect His plan in my life. The thing we must not do is let our sinful condition turn us from God. Though redeemed by grace, we are flawed creatures, and there will be times we desire something outside God's plan for us. At these times, we may not understand God or His commands. The choice before us is to cave to our feelings, or recognize a greater truth exists beyond what we feel. Struggles and doubts may come, but we must seek our answers with God, not outside of Him (or we will end up with a solution outside of Him, which is no solution at all). There are things about us we cannot fix ourselves. As believers, we must turn to God – not after we have cleaned ourselves, for that is impossible – but come to Him in our mess.

Sexual sins especially are so personal it can seem impossible to separate the sin and the sinner, but your sin does not define you; you are defined by your relationship as a child of God. A sexuality that is confused and broken (a natural ramification of this fallen world!) may demonstrate itself in a variety of equally wrong manifestations: lust outside of a marriage relationship, fornication, adultery, masturbation, pornography (including "chick flick" sex scenes), homosexual desires or relations. Regardless of your personal struggles and sins, they do not define you; your core identity is not a "fornicator," a "lesbian," etc.; if you are a Christian, your core identity is still that you are a child of God.

In all this talk of grace, we must not lose sight of the fact that God is holy, and cannot approve of any kind of sin (Isa. 57:15; 1 Pet. 1:15-16; Rev. 4:8). God's clear design in Scripture is for one man and one woman to come together in marriage (Gen. 1:27, 2:24; Mark 10:7-8; Eph. 5:31). Sexual activity of any nature outside of this is forbidden (Rom. 1:24-32; 1 Cor. 6:18-19; Eph. 5:3-5; 1 Thess. 4:3). A person is not determined by how they have been born or how circumstances shape them; we are responsible for what we do with our emotions and feelings. Will you, out of love for God, bring yours into submission to His plan? This is a living sacrifice, an acceptable act of worship (Rom. 12:1-2). As we adhere to this, we find true freedom comes through surrender to God's best plan. The will of God is indeed *good*, and *acceptable*, and *perfect* (Rom. 12:2).

To return to the gospel, we know God uses the relationship between a husband and a wife as an illustration of Christ and the Church (Eph. 5:22-33). Of course, the union between Christ and His Church is not sexual, but correlations can be drawn. In a marriage relationship, the woman opens herself up to receive and the man enters, and life is given. This is a figure of the gospel, and this is why sexual deviations are an affront to God. These ruin the imagery of the gospel (and are, in fact, often associated with false gospels, e.g. 2 Pet. 2:14).

There are two main approaches to moral purity, involving either external restraints or internal motivations. Lawrence Woo offers the following illustration of the sirens from Greek mythology.[6] These creatures are described in the *Dictionary of Classical Mythology* as "singing enchantresses who lured men to their death."[7] They destroyed all those foolish enough to sail by their territory, except for two men: Odysseus and Jason. In his voyages, Odysseus was required to cross by the shores of the sirens. His solution was to put beeswax in the ears of his crew, who continued to row the ship, unaware of the music of the sirens. Odysseus, however, wanted to experience this fabled wonder.

He also wanted to live, so he had his crew bind him to the mast of the ship. He heard the beautiful song of the sirens, but try as he would to join them, he could not break his bonds, and he and his (still oblivious) crew sailed by safely. Odysseus knew his weakness, and he knew a personal battle lay ahead, and his solution was to invoke external restraints so that it would be impossible for him to fulfill his misguided desires.

The other ship to avoid the trap of the sirens was manned by Jason and the Argonauts, but Jason elected a different stratagem than the one Odysseus would adopt. Instead, Jason brought with him the most skillful musician of Greek legend, a man by the name of Orpheus. As the sirens began their song, Orpheus played his own, more beautiful music, and Jason and his crew, enraptured by the better song, were immune to the charms of the sirens.

As Christians, we can put external restraints on our sinful cravings, but neither the commandments of God (which ought to be obeyed) nor the legalism of man (which we would do well to disregard) will change our desire, for if the bonds that confine us to the mast could be broken, we would be out among the sirens in a moment. However, communion with the Lord drives away the thirst for sinful things. If our heart is taken up with the "better song," both our actions and our desires will be marked by purity. Remember, no human relationship offers complete fulfillment; you must seek satisfaction in Christ.

God does not leave us without hope in this battle. In one of his letters to the Corinthians, Paul included both a warning and a promise:

> *Therefore let him who thinks he stands take heed lest he fall. No temptation has overtaken you except such as is common to man; but God is faithful, who will not allow you to be tempted beyond what you are able, but with the temptation will also make the way of escape, that you may be able to bear it* (1 Cor. 10:12-13).

God promises a way out or a way to overcome each temptation that faces us. We are not alone; He is more committed to our purity than we are!

When we decide to side with God on the matter of moral purity, this is a way to show our love for Him, and to glorify Him in our lives. God could have instantly eradicated our flesh nature when He justified us, but He didn't, and that tells me there is value in the war with sin, that is, in learning to yield to God's Word and to rest in His grace. So take heart. Approached in the correct manner, this can increase our dependence on God and actually deepen our relationship with Him. The lessons we learn in this effort for purity are applicable across a variety of situations, and may enable us to help and be a blessing to others.

Emotional Promiscuity and Mental Purity

A Christian woman, single or not, must be committed to the personal discipline of purity; this encompasses much more than merely avoiding sexual immorality. The "Proverbs 7 Woman," in contrast to the "Proverbs 31 Woman," shows us women can establish an environment where men are either motivated to be morally pure or where they are tempted to indulge in immorality. Therefore, it is important to be modest in one's comportment, conversation, and attire. You would not want your brothers in Christ to defraud you by paying special attention to single women they do not intend to marry, so do not defraud them by dressing or behaving provocatively.

God created man to be the initiator and woman to be the responder in a couple's relationship. We see this all the way back to the story of Adam and Eve. Thus, women do not need to worry about finding a mate. If you want to get married badly enough, I dare say you could manage it. However, the actions of Sarah when she gave Hagar to Abraham, and of Rebecca when she and Jacob tricked Isaac, teach us that you will suffer if you take things out of God's hands and into your own. At the very least, you will miss out on God's best. Instead, focus on walking faithfully with the Lord; if He wants you married, He is able to arrange the details in His own way, in His own time!

But waiting is hard. Jim Elliot, who held off marrying Elisabeth until (and if) such a time arose that their marriage would promote their service for God and not distract from it, described the process as "waiting on Him for whom it is no vain thing to wait."[8] For those trusting God with a hope deferred, Matthew Henry has the following encouragement:

> Cast not away your confidence because God defers His performances. That which does not come in your time, will be hastened in His time, which is always the more convenient season. God will work when He pleases, how He pleases, and by what means He pleases. He is not

bound to keep our time, but He will perform His word, honor our faith, and reward them that diligently seek Him.[9]

It is highly important for Christian women to be content, pure, and disciplined. I think we have all seen failures in this area. One of the more subtle ways a person can fall short is through *emotional* promiscuity. Recall that in chapter ten we examined the importance of a protected heart (Prov. 4:23). The heart is protected by keeping God's Word in it, by putting away iniquity, by having the proper focus and direction, and by prayer and thanksgiving. We were warned not to let desires become demands, which lead to disappointment. Rather, we are to accept God's gifts with thanksgiving. God's own peace will guard our hearts as we exercise faith, gratitude, and contentment (Phil. 4:6-7). We also examined some of the symptoms and results of "mental dating." This happens when people, who may recognize the problems associated with the casual dating routine and want to avoid a series of relationships that foster intimacy without commitment, instead turn to concocting hypothetical romantic scenarios in their minds. It is possible to be promiscuous while maintaining an outward display of purity when the promiscuity is emotional rather than physical. F. B. Meyer cautions:

> It is as ruinous to indulge the desires of the *mind* as those of the *flesh*. By the marvelous gift of imagination we may indulge unholy fantasies, and throw the reins on the neck of the steeds of passion – always stopping short of the act. No human eye follows the soul when it goes forth to dance with satyrs or to thread the labyrinthine maze of the islands of desire. It goes and returns unsuspected by the nearest. Its credit for snow-white purity is not forfeited. It is still permitted to watch among the virgins for the Bridegroom's advent. But if this practice is unjudged and unconfessed, it marks the offender a son of disobedience and a child of wrath.[10]

Apart from Christ, all our righteous deeds – as well as emotions, resolutions, and thoughts – are filthy rags (Isa. 64:6). Scripture indicates purity is more than physical: Jeremiah 17:9 tells us the *heart* is naturally wicked, while Proverbs 4:23, as we have seen, indicates the need to guard the heart. Remember the heart is the core of personality and involves one's morality, emotions, will, and cognition. Also recall the Greek word used to signify purity is *katharos* and it means freedom "from corrupt desire, from sin and guilt."[11] Purity does not just relate to actions, but also to desires.

I think most Christian women (even those who view movies with "occasional" pornographic scenes!) would look down on a Christian man who dallied in pornography. However, before we look down our noses too sharply, let us consider whether our own hearts be so unsullied. Oh no, you say, I have no desire to look at such trash! That may be, but is this due to a truly pure heart, or perhaps only to differences in areas of weakness? Might there be something else infecting your own heart and mind? Generally speaking, men have greater visual and physical needs while women have greater tactile and emotional needs. Whether a man lusts after the physical relationship or a woman lusts after the emotional relationship – are not both in sin? I do not mean to excuse the men, but to challenge the women: as one young Christian woman has said, "Just because you aren't thinking about fornication does not ensure that your thoughts are pure. Not having God-honoring thoughts is spiritual adultery."[12] This occurs whenever we are distracted away from our First Love.

Care must be taken to avoid "emotional promiscuity." What is meant by this term? To look at a young man in your life and to imagine dating him, what he would say to you and what you would say back to him, what you might do and where you might go with him, the flowers he would buy, the moments you would share – in short, to fabricate a romance in your mind – this is sin. To repeat the process is promiscuity.

At the very least, emotional promiscuity involves a lack of contentment (which is idolatry, Eph. 5:5), if not outright lust (which is adultery, Matt. 5:28). It hinders spiritual growth and fosters abnormal relationships. Emotional promiscuity leaves the heart unguarded, allowing thoughts to ultimately proceed to actions. Desire changes to demand, with its expectations of fulfillment, and then leads to disappointment. This pattern sets a person up for disappointment in other relationships and other areas of life.

But what should we do with the distraction of attraction? Let's say you're committed to purity and you have a heart for God, but there's a guy you can't seem to get out of your head. What to do? Leslie Ludy has the following to say:

131

Being attracted to a guy isn't wrong in itself; it's a natural part of the way that God made us. But if we don't handle attraction correctly, it can also become one of the most dangerous stumbling blocks to our spiritual walk. If you allow attraction toward a guy to overtake your thoughts and emotions, it can easily become an idol in your life that is taking your focus off Christ. Attraction can quickly morph into an unhealthy emotional obsession with someone – clouding your relationship with your King and dishonoring your relationship with your future husband.[13]

There is a difference between attraction and infatuation; the former could just be noticing someone's good qualities, while the latter is allowing someone to displace God as the focus of your affection. It is a form of idolatry, a work of the flesh. Infatuation is when you let imagination carry you away, and it is fed on daydreams, looking through photos, juicy gossip sessions with your friends, etc. As such, infatuation is typically an illusion; how many times have you found someone is not quite like you dreamed him to be? It is alright to appreciate someone without elevating that person above Christ in your heart; however, too often we must echo the psalmist's prayer: *"Give me an undivided heart"* (Ps. 86:11, NIV). The trick is not to let *attraction* become *distraction*.

The Pursuit of Purity

There are at least five activities that will help us to control romantic notions or emotions: make Christ your first love, surrender the matter to Him, take every thought captive, stay busy, and allow for divine intervention.

First, make Christ your first love. The way forward is to repent, come clean, and have a heart that is captivated by Christ: *"Draw near to God and He will draw near to you. Cleanse your hands, you sinners; and purify your hearts, you double minded"* (Jas. 4:8). To guard your heart effectively, you must spend time alone in the quietness of His presence. God is my strength, my hope, my joy, and my ultimate reward. He is the source of my satisfaction. He is to be my one love.

Second, if you find an attraction is fast becoming a distraction, surrender it into God's hands as a way of guarding your heart from infatuation. We believe God is all-powerful, don't we? We believe He loves us and wants the best for us, don't we? Then let Him write your life's story. It is not permissible to dwell on a hypothetical scenario, however godly the young man in question appears. As one young woman writes, "We set ourselves up for disappointment, regret, and heartache when we allow this to happen, and yes, we do allow it to happen. As promised in 1 Corinthians 10:13, we can be sure that there is a way of escape for every temptation that we encounter."[14] Let your mind dwell on what is true.

Third, exercise godly integrity in your mind by taking every thought captive. *The Scottish Chiefs* describes the thoughts of the character Helen upon meeting William Wallace: "Not to think of him was impossible. How to think of him was within her own power."[15] Helen knew there was a difference between noticing someone's good qualities and obsessing about the person himself. It has been said we are not responsible for the birds that fly past our heads, but we are accountable for those that make a nest in our hair. Thoughts will fly through our minds, but don't allow foolish ones to "build a nest" there! Do not milk a crush. You will not get past an obsession about a particular young man by creeping on his Facebook page each day or being on text alert for his social media accounts or otherwise contriving "chance" encounters to run into each other.

Be conscious of the divine surveillance of your thought life. If, in cartoon fashion, your thoughts could be read in a bubble above your head, would others consider these appropriate, edifying, and God-honoring? This is thankfully a hypothetical situation; however, our thoughts influence the visible aspects of our lives more than we'd like to think. In any case, be sure the way you think about a guy does not betray his (potential) future wife or your (potential) future husband. Honor the Lord in your thought life!

Anchor your mind in truth; Paul tells us, *"Finally, brethren, whatever things are true, whatever things are noble, whatever things are just, whatever things are pure, whatever things are lovely, whatever things are of good report, if there is any virtue and if there is anything praiseworthy—meditate on these things"* (Phil. 4:8). Do not allow your thoughts to jump ahead of what he really said, what he really did to create a mental fairytale with no basis in reality. What you think about will affect your perception and behavior and relationships. God knows your thoughts, and you are responsible for them.

Fourth, when you recognize you are starting to let infatuation have a stronghold in your mind, channel your energy into something productive. It's a funny thing about one's mind: it can only focus well on one thing at a time. Something always comes to fill up the spaces, whether we are talking of one's heart or mind or time. If your heart and mind are full of the Lord, you are less likely to be distracted by a mere mortal. If your time is full in the work of the Lord, you are less likely to sink to self-pity or discontentment.

Find ways to utilize this season of your life. Be faithful and content with current obligations. As F.B. Meyer so aptly put it, "How often we ask God for wider spheres of usefulness, whilst we fail to utilize those which lie within our reach."[16] Don't complain or have a negative attitude. Guard your tongue. Be a good communicator. Don't shut people out by letting one individual define your world; take the initiative to reach out to others. Invest in others: pray for them, encourage them, serve them. Stay busy in the service of the Lord. Study God's Word and deepen your relationship with God. Exercise personal discipline. Keep an attitude of willing obedience to God, humility, industriousness, contentment, hopefulness, and joy. Whenever you start to dream about a young man, use it as a reminder to turn to prayer (it's probably wise to pray for people other than the guy in question!) or to memorize, review, and meditate on Scripture. Avoid areas of weakness and guard your behavior and speech. Instead, pour out your heart to the Lord.

Fifth, there is another action you may need to take against an infatuation. Even amidst the best of intentions, crushes die hard. One of my close friends, who would very much like to be married to a godly man, once told me that when she seems unable to get a guy out of her head even though it appears it is not God's will, or at least not His timing, to pursue marriage (i.e. the young man in question does not express interest), she prays for the Lord to bring something about that will take away her obsession. She warns not to pray this lightly, as sometimes it seems that drastic action is needed on the part of the Lord to cut something like this out of one's heart. But she also says this prayer has always been effective, the mental fantasy removed, joyful undistracted service for the Lord resumed, and I have found this to be true in my own life also.

Summary

So how, then, ought we to conduct ourselves in the time of our earthly sojourn? It is important, once we have committed to emotional purity, not to relapse into bad habits. Bethany Juedes offers the following encouragements:

- Don't allow secret sin to fester. If confessing it to the Lord does not prevent you from continuously repeating the same sin, ask a trusted believer to help keep you accountable.
- Find an accountability partner who isn't a matchmaker. Someone who has your best in mind will not try to "solve your problem" according to man's way by gossiping and speculating about who might be a good match for you. This undermines God's purpose for your present state of singleness.
- Pray for God to redirect your thoughts each time you are tempted (1 Cor. 10:13). Since this prayer agrees with God's standard for purity, He is more than pleased to grant this request, but we need to take Him up on this offer and forsake the sinful pattern. We can't expect the Lord to preserve us from harm when we willingly allow ourselves to ponder the very sin He prohibits.
- Don't tease fellow single women about men, especially about a certain man. Don't tempt your sisters that the Lord is "sending a sign of confirmation" that this person is "the one." You don't know what mental battle she is struggling in. The Lord does not reveal His will through the avenue of gossip. Women can fall into the trap of spiritualizing their inappropriate expectations as "God's will" because they were fueled by Christian friends who were probably not exercised of the Lord to encourage you concerning a certain man...
- Don't ignore men; this does not solve the underlying problem. Instead, ask God to help you act normally around godly men. Don't be a husband hunter or a man dodger. View them as brothers in Christ, not prospective husbands. Adopting God's perspective on the situation is the solution.
- Do not slander men in an effort to make sure others know you are uninterested. This is sin as well.
- Take everything to God in prayer. Make life one long, continuous conversation with your heavenly Father.
- Thank God for the time during your singleness to have the defects in your character worked out, lest your husband would have met

you earlier and have been turned off by your flaws. This is not to say that married women have arrived at optimum spiritual capacity, for the Lord gives wives to men as He sees fit, not as we deserve.[17]

In summary, be neither a husband-hunter nor a man-dodger. Enjoy the relationships and opportunities God has currently placed in your life. Be committed to honoring God, not just in your behavior and speech, but also in your thoughts and emotions. May He ever be first in your life, and may there be no "close seconds." Our God is the Most Holy One; may we be holy in all aspects of our lives and committed to both physical and mental purity.

When you have no helpers, see your helpers in God. When you have many helpers, see God in all your helpers. When you have nothing but God, see all in God. When you have everything, see God in everything. Under all conditions, stay thy heart only on the Lord.

— Charles Surgeon[18]

Note: I suggest those interested in further study on this subject would benefit from: *Singled Out for Him* (Nancy Leigh DeMoss), *I Kissed Dating Goodbye* (Joshua Harris), *Did I Kiss Marriage Goodbye?* (Carolyn McCulley), and *The Path of Loneliness* (Elisabeth Elliot).

Conclusion

Keep your heart with all diligence, for out of it spring the issues of life.
(Prov. 4:23)

All the issues of life are truly rooted in the heart; it affects what we think, say, do, and who we are as individuals. In the first portion of this book, *The Issues of Life - The Heart of the Matter*, we learned the heart is the center of personality and involves the emotions, moral character, will, and cognition. We also looked at foundational matters such as God's claim to our heart and our need for a heart like God's heart. In the second section, *Your Heart - The Anatomy of a Spiritual Heart*, we took a closer look at the type of heart that delights God and found Scripture describes it as one that is penitent, pure, perfect, prepared, purposed, and protected. In the final portion of this book, *With All Diligence - Disciplines of the Heart*, we examined various disciplines of the heart: self-control, contentment, thankfulness, faithfulness, joy, patience, submission, prayer, and purity.

These exercises help us guard our heart in a manner that is honoring to the Lord. For the Christian, discipline is crucial, even in the little things of life. As Leonard Ravenhill states, "How can you pull down strongholds of Satan if you don't even have the strength to turn off your TV?"[1] Or, as Keith Green colorfully sang, "Jesus rose from the dead, and you, you can't even get out of bed!"[2] Let us come before the Lord and confess our lack of discipline and pray for His strength as we endeavor to keep our hearts, and lives, with diligence.

I can think of no better way to conclude this sketch of the heart than with the exhortation John recorded at the close of his first epistle: *"Little children, keep yourselves from idols. Amen"* (1 Jn. 5:21). John Calvin referred to human nature as a "perpetual factory of idols."[3] Watch out for them! An idol is anything that robs our love, time, or attention from the Lord Jesus Christ. Idols may seem harmless, fun, and exciting – but they will drain you. Lord, rid my heart from all attractions; rid my mind of all distractions, beside You. I want You to be my one love.

We say "one love" but a true love for Christ will spill over into sacrificial love for others. Love is not a limited quality, where one recipient loses if another has more. Loving increases love's capacity. If you love Christ above everything, you will be filled with peace, joy, and love for others. Conversely, if you love a person above Christ, you will be unable to truly love him or her as you should, as C. S. Lewis explains:

> When I have learnt to love God better than my earthly dearest, I shall love my earthly dearest better than I do now. Insofar as I learn to love my earthly dearest at the expense of God and instead of God, I shall be moving towards the state in which I shall not love my earthly dearest at all. When first things are put first, second things are not suppressed but increased.[4]

Idolatry is a work of the flesh, but love is a fruit of the Spirit (Gal. 5). The problem is we love too little; what we call "love" is often selfish, laced with our own expectations. Or the problem is that our love too easily becomes idolatry. What is needed is a consuming passion for Christ, and then we will have a Christlike love for others.

Let us look at the example provided for us in the nation of Israel around the time of their Babylonian captivity. Instead of identifying with the Lord, the Jews had forsaken Him and His Word (Jer. 9:13). A void exists in the human heart that only God can satisfy; forsaking Him necessitates an attempt to fill that emptiness with something else; the Jews chose to replace Jehovah with the worship of Baal and the dictates of their own hearts: *"...they have forsaken My law which I set before them, and have not obeyed My voice...but have walked after the imagination of their own heart..."* (Jer. 9:13-14, KJV). While it is true that most Christians will not create idols of stone and wood to worship, we are prone to engage in materialism or mental fabrications which then replace the Lord's rightful place in our hearts. However, the "imaginations" of our own hearts are destructive, and poor substitutes for the reality of a life lived for God.

Throughout the Bible (and history), idolatry is shown to be an open door to immorality. It is therefore pertinent for us to again recall John's parting exhortation to fellow believers, *"keep yourselves from idols"* (1

Jn. 5:21). Idols in our hearts will eventually lead us into moral ruin. Guard your heart – watch out for idols!

> The dearest idol I have known,
> Whate'er that idol be,
> Help me to tear it from Thy throne,
> And worship only Thee.

> — William Cowper[5]

Endnotes

Introduction

Does God Have Your Heart?
1. "Redeem," *Dictionary.com Unabridged* (Random House, Inc.), accessed June 20, 2014, http://dictionary.reference.com/browse/redeem.
2. Jabe Nicholson, *"The Desire, Diet, and Direction of My Soul"* (Presentation, Vessels of Honor Conference: Parkville, MO, May 2009), Mp3, 0:19:22, accessed June 14, 2014, http://www.westsidebiblechapel.net/Conferences/2009Vessels.html.

Falling in Love With the Lord
1. Matthew Jordan Henderson, *"Prayer"* (Presentation, River Valley Christian Fellowship: Chippewa Falls, WI, 2011).
2. Mathew Henry, *Matthew Henry's Commentary of the Whole Bible 9.x* (n.p., 1706: e-Sword module created by Rick Meyers, 2013), sec. 1 Thessalonians 5:16-22.
3. Leslie Ludy, "The Art of Sacred Living." *Set Apart Girl,* Sep/Oct 2012, 76. Accessed on June 14, 2014, http://setapartgirl.com/magazine/issue/2012/sep-oct.
4. Henry, *Matthew Henry's Commentary*, sec. Deuteronomy 6:4-16.
5. Ibid., sec. Mark 12:28-34.

What Is the Heart?
1. Warren Henderson, *Forsaken, Forgotten, and Forgiven* (Warren A. Henderson Publishing, 2012), 139.
2. Warren Henderson, *Mindframes* (Port Colborne, ON: Gospel Folio Press, 2004), 138.
3. Henderson, *Forsaken, Forgotten, and Forgiven*, 139.
4. Henderson, *Mindframes,* 139.
5. Henderson, *Forsaken, Forgotten, and Forgiven*, 139.
6. Gerald Cowen, "Mind," in Holman's Bible Dictionary, ed. Trent Butler (Broadman & Holman, 1991) accessed July 30, 2014, http://www.studylight.org/dictionaries/hbd/view.cgi?n=4326.
7. Augustine, Confessions (Indianapolis, IN: Hackett Publishing Company, 2006), 3, accessed October 8, 2014, books.google.com/books?isbn=1603845712.

A Heart After God's Own Heart

1. George Herbert, quoted in "George Herbert on God," *oChristian.com,* accessed June 14, 2014, http://christian-quotes.ochristian.com/christian-quotes_ochristian.cgi?find=Christian-quotes-by-George+Herbert-on-God.
2. These notes are taken from Scott DeGroff, *"Discerning the Will of God"* (Presentation, Vessels of Honor Conference: Parkville, MO, 2010), Mp3, accessed September 16, 2014, http://www.westsidebiblechapel.net/Conferences/2010Vessels.htm.
3. "History," *Samaritan's Purse,* accessed June 14, 2014, http://www.samaritanspurse.org/index.php/Who_We_Are/History.

The Penitent Heart

1. "Penitent," *Dictionary.com Unabridged* (Random House, Inc.), accessed June 14, 2014, http://dictionary.reference.com/browse/penitent.
2. Henry, *Matthew Henry's Commentary*, sec. Hebrew 10:19-39.
3. J. Vernon McGee, "Hosea Study Guide: Introduction," from *Thru the Bible Commentary, Vol. 27: Hosea & Joel* (Nashville, TN: Thomas Nelson Publishers, 1991), accessed August 5, 2014, http://www.ttb.org/contentpages.aspx?viewcontentpageguid=f1c4fb49-01e2-4650-a734-9e3e3c54b77b&parentnavigationid=21792.
4. John Bunyan, *The Whole Works of John Bunyan, Reprinted, Volume I,* reprinted by George Offor (London: Blackie and Son, Paternoster Row, 1862), *cxv,* e-book accessed June 20, 2014, books.google.com/books?id=Ns4GAAAAYAAJ.

The Pure Heart

1. Richard Cowen, "Chapter 6: Ancient Silver and Gold," in *Exploiting the Earth* (Essay, UC Davis), last modified April 1999, http://mygeologypage.ucdavis.edu/cowen/~gel115/115CH6.html.
2. The NKJV of John 15:2 reads, *"Every branch in Me that does not bear fruit He takes away...."* The Greek word for "takes away" is *airo* and Thayer defines this as "1) to raise up, elevate, lift up...2) to take upon one's self and carry what has been raised up, to bear 3) to bear away what has been raised, carry off..." (Thayer, *Thayer's Greek Definitions,* G142, airo). The context of this passage would indicate the branch represents a Christian (the Lord is speaking to His disciples, and states the branch in question is *"in Me"*). The passage does not teach, as has been supposed, that Christians can lose their salvation if they fail to bring forth spiritual fruit; we know from the whole of Scripture that the believer is eternally secure. Rather, John 15 teaches our need to be pruned, cleansed, and to abide in Christ in order to have a life marked by spiritual fruit. It is the author's opinion that in this context *"lifts up"* is a better translation of the Greek word *airo*, and indicates the Lord will work in the lives of fruitless believers, to "lift" them out of the world's mud and raise them up to a position of fruitfulness in the Lord.

The Pure Heart (cont.)
3. Joseph Henry Thayer, *Thayer's Greek Definitions 9.x, (Thayer's Greek-English Lexicon of the New Testament,* Hendrickson Publishers, n.d.: e-Sword module created by Rick Meyer, 2009), G2513 katharos.
4. Henry, *Matthew Henry's Commentary*, sec. Hebrews 10:19-39.
5. Duncan Campbell, quoted in "Heart Purity," *oChristian.com*, accessed June 14, 2014, http://articles.ochristian.com/article10393.shtml.
6. Dwight L. Moody, *Notes from My Bible: From Genesis to Revelation* (Chicago, IL: Fleming H Revell Co., 1895), 8, e-book accessed June 20, 2014, books.google.com/books?id=0lYkxPZAY4AC.
7. Charles Spurgeon, quoted in "Charles Spurgeon on Holiness," *oChristian.com,* accessed June 14, 2014, http://christian-quotes.ochristian.com/christian-quotes_ochristian.cgi?find=Christian-quotes-by-Charles+Spurgeon-on-Holiness.

The Perfect Heart
1. James Strong, *Strong's with Tense Voice and Mood (Strong's Hebrew and Greek Dictionaries,* n.p. 1890: e-Sword module created 2009), H8003 shalem.

The Prepared Heart
1. Strong, *Strong's with Tense Voice and Mood*, H3559 kun.
2. Brian Edwards, *Revival! A People Saturated with God* (Darlington, England: Evangelical Press, 1990), 120.

The Purposed Heart
1. Strong, *Strong's with Tense Voice and Mood*, G4286 prothesis.
2. Carolyn McCulley, *Did I Kiss Marriage Goodbye?*, 44.
3. Lee Weber, *"Psalm 101: A Vow for a Holy Life"* (Presentation, River Valley Christian Fellowship: Chippewa Falls, WI, 2010).
4. Harry A. Ironside, *Daniel* (Neptune, NJ: Loizeaux Brothers, revised ed. 1996), 27.

The Protected Heart
1. Kathryn L. McCance, "Structure and Function of the Cardiovascular and Lymphatic Systems," in *Pathophysiology: The Biologic Basis for Disease in Adults and Children, 5th ed.*, ed Kathryn L. McCance & Sue Huether (St. Louis, MO: Elsevier Mosby, 2006), 1031.
2. *Taber's Cyclopedic Medical Dictionary*, 20th ed., ed. Dr. Donald Venes (Philadelphia, PA: F. A. Davis, 2001), 940.
3. Henry, Matthew Henry's Commentary, sec. Proverbs 4:20-27.
4. Ibid.
5. Oswald Chambers, quoted in *Great-Quotes.com*, accessed July 30, 2014, http://www.great-quotes.com/quotes/author/Oswald/Chambers.
6. Carolyn McCulley, *Did I Kiss Marriage Goodbye?*, 78-79.

The Protected Heart (cont.)

7. Paul David Tripp, *Instruments in the Redeemer's Hands* (Phillipsburg, NJ: P&R Publishers, 2002), 85-88, quoted in Carolyn McCulley, *Did I Kiss Marriage Goodbye? Trusting God with a Hope Deferred* (Wheaton, IL: Crossway Books, 2004), 79.
8. Robert Murray McCheyne, "A Voice from the Past: Look and Live!" *Journal of the Grace Evangelical Society*, Spring 1992, Vol. 5:1 (Irving, TX: Grace Evangelical Society), accessed July 29, 2014, www.faithalone.org/journal/1992i/McChey.html.
9. Henry, Matthew Henry's Commentary, sec. Proverbs 4:20-27.
10. Charles Wesley, "I Want a Heart to Pray," *Wesley Center Online*, accessed June 20, 2014, http://wesley.nnu.edu/?id=4446.

Personal Discipline

1. "Discipline," *Dictionary.com Unabridged* (Random House, Inc.), accessed July 17, 2011, http://dictionary.reference.com/browse/discipline.
2. Elisabeth Elliot, *Dicipline: The Glad Surrender* (Grand Rapids, MI: Revell, 1982), 22.
3. Strong, *Strong's with Tense Voice and Mood*, G1128 *gumnazō*.
4. Jabe Nicholson, *"What did Jesus Expect the Church to be?"* (Presentation, Vessels of Honor Conference: Parkville, MO, 2009), Mp3, 00:09:42, accessed June 14, 2014, http://www.westsidebiblechapel.net/Conferences/2009Vessels.htm.

The Discipline of Self-Control

1. "Self-control," *Collins English Dictionary - Complete & Unabridged*, 10th ed., (HarperCollins Publishers), accessed April 24, 2013, http://dictionary.reference.com/browse/self-control.
2. Nancy Rolinger, *The Fruit of the Spirit: Self-Control* (Audio Bible study), Mp3, 21:26, accessed October 9, 2014, https://www.dropbox.com/sh/29c59ejdhdui48l/AABn-eLCTDikDAJOieoS9Gz1a/titus_woman/audio/2002titus04.mp3?dl=0.
3. Cynthia L. McClurg, "Don't Let Your Mind Go Awandering," in *Growing Songs for Children, Vol. 2* (Warrenton, MO: Child Evangelism Fellowship Press, 1992), song 56.
4. Nancy Rolinger, *Be a Quality Woman, Lesson #4* (Bible study handout), 2, pdf, accessed October 9, 2014, https://www.dropbox.com/sh/29c59ejdhdui48l/AAD0k6QflvXdh0RU7ALCfHhda/titus_woman/handouts/04questions.pdf?dl=0.
5. Elliot, *Discipline: The Glad Surrender*, 138.
6. Strong, *Strong's with Tense Voice and Mood*, H3559 kun.
7. Elliot, *Discipline: The Glad Surrender*, 133.
8. Ibid, 141-142.
9. Ann Voscamp, *One Thousand Gifts* (Grand Rapids, MI: Zondervan, 2010), 146.

The Discipline of Self-Control (cont.)

10. Ibid, 148.
11. Ibid, 136.
12. Strong, *Strong's with Tense Voice and Mood*, G692 argos.
13. Rolinger, *Be a Quality Woman, Lesson #4*, 2, emphasis removed.
14. Brian Gunning, *The Church at Work: 40 practical blueprints for working with the Master Builder* (Port Colborne, ON: Gospel Folio Press, 2000), 33.
15. Elliot, *Discipline: The Glad Surrender*, 44.
16. William MacDonald, *The Disciple's Manual* (Port Colborne, ON: Gospel Folio Press, 2004), 285.
17. Bunyan, *The Whole Works*, cxxiii.
18. George Muller, *The Autobiography of George Muller* (New Kensington, PA: Whitaker House, 1984), 118.
19. A. W. Tozer - Summarized in *Choice Gleanings*: November 20, 2006 (Port Colborne, ON: Gospel Folio Press, 2006).

The Discipline of Contentment

1. Aaron R. Wolfe, "Complete in Thee," in *Hymns of Worship and Remembrance* (Fort Dodge, IA: Gospel Perpetuating Publishers, 1971), hymn 414.
2. "Contentment." *Easton's 1897 Bible Dictionary*, accessed March 14, 2011, http://dictionary.reference.com/browse/contentment.
3. Charles H. Spurgeon, *"Holy Water"* (Presentation, The Metropolitan Tabernacle: Newington, November 8, 1874), 4, accessed June 20, 2014, http://www.spurgeongems.org/vols19-21/chs1202.pdf.
4. Thayer, *Thayer's Greek Definitions,* G3499, nekroo.
5. Henderson, *Forsaken, Forgotten, and Forgiven*, 130.
6. Ibid, 113.
7. Amy Carmichael, "Rose from Brier" in *The Collected Poems of Amy Carmichael: Mountain Breezes* (Fort Washington, PA: Christian Literature Crusade, 1999), 294.

The Discipline of Thankfulness

1. Elisabeth Elliot, quoted in "Gratitude," *Photos, Hodgepodge, and Miscellany* (January 13, 2012). Accessed October 9, 2014, https://billydie.wordpress.com/tag/elisabeth-elliot.
2. Dr. John G. Mitchel, quoted in Ruth Myers and Warren Myers, *31 Days of Praise* (Colorado Springs, CO: Multnomah Books, 1994), 26.
3. Myers, *31 Days of Praise*, 26-27.
4. Ibid, 28.
5. William Shakespeare, *Henry VI*, Part 2, act 1, sc. 1, l. 19-20, accessed July 29, 2014, http://www.online-literature.com/shakespeare/henryVI2/2/.

The Discipline of Faithfulness
1. Oswald Chambers, quoted in *Great-Quotes.com*, accessed July 30, 2014, http://www.great-quotes.com/quotes/author/Oswald/Chambers.
2. Carl Knot, "April 4, 2013" in *2013 Choice Gleanings Calendar* (Port Colborne, Ontario: Gospel Folio Press, 2013).
3. Joe Reese, *"Be Careful About the Little Things"* (Presentation, Vessels of Honor Conference: Parkville, MO, 2010), Mp3, 0:08:29, accessed June 14, 2014, http://www.westsidebiblechapel.net/Conferences/2010Vessels.htm.
4. Oswald Chambers, "December 18," *My Upmost for His Highest, updated edition* (Discovery House Publishers, October 2010), accessed July 30, 2014, http://utmost.org/test-of-faithfulness/.

The Discipline of Joy
1. William MacDonald, *Believer's Bible Commentary*, ed. Arthur Farstad (Nashville, TN: Thomas Nelson Publishers, 1989), 1894.
2. Anonymous, "Behold, A Spotless Victim Dies," *Hymns of Worship*, hymn 147.
3. Michael Card, "Could It Be?" *Present Reality* (Sparrow Records, 1988), CD.
4. Billy Sunday, quoted in *oChristian.com*, accessed July 30, 2014, http://christian-quotes.ochristian.com/Billy-Sunday-Quotes/page-5.shtml.
5. Warren Henderson, *Exploring the Pauline Epistles – Bible Study Helps* (e-book, Warren A Henderson publishing; 2008), 363.
6. Voscamp, *One Thousand Gifts*, 166.
7. Ibid, 176.
8. Henry, *Matthew Henry's Commentary,* sec. Nehemiah 8:9-12.

The Discipline of Patience
1. Strong, *Strong's with Tense Voice and Mood*, G5281 hupomone.
2. Charles Randall Barnes, *The People's Bible Encyclopedia* (Chicago, IL: The People's Publication Society, 1912), 831, accessed October 9, 2014, books.google.com/books?id=-CsVAAAAYAAJ.
3. Elisabeth Elliot, *Keep a Quiet Heart* (Grand Rapids, MI: Revell, 1995), 135.
4. Ibid, 136.
5. Jean-Pierre de Caussade, quoted in *A Guide to Prayer for All God's People*, Rueben Job and Norman Shawchuck, eds. (Nashville, TN: Upper Room, 1990), 244.
6. Hudson Taylor, quoted in *oChristian.com*, accessed July 30, 2014, http://christian-quotes.ochristian.com/Patience-Quotes/page-3.shtml.
7. Warren Wiersbe, quoted in *oChristian*.com, accessed July 30, 2014, http://christian-quotes.ochristian.com/Patience-Quotes/page-3.shtml

The Discipline of Submission
1. Strong, *Strong's with Tense Voice and Mood*, G5293 hupotasso.
2. Augustine, *Confessions*, 3.
3. C. T. Studd, quoted in Norman Grubb, *C. T. Studd: Cricketer and Pioneer* (Fort Washington, PA: CLC Publications, 1933, 2012), 124.

The Discipline of Submission (cont.)

4. Samuel Zwemer, "The Glory of the Impossible" in *Perspectives on the World Christian Movement,* Ralph Winter and Stephen Hawthorne, eds. (Pasadena, CA: William Carey Library, 1981), 259.

5. William MacDonald, *True Discipleship,* (Port Colborne, ON: Gospel Folio Press, 1962), 25.

6. Jim Elliot, *The Journals of Jim Elliot,* ed. Elisabeth Elliot (Grand Rapids, MI: Revell, Baker Publishing Group 1978), 174.

7. Andrew Reed "Spirit Divine" in *The Hymnal, Revised and Enlarged: Episcopal Church* (New York, NY: Oxford University Press, 1892), hymn 382, accessed July 30, 2014, books.google.com/books?id=wDk3AAAAMAAJ.

8. Harriet Eleanor Baillie-Hamilton King, *Ugo Bassi's Sermon in the Hospital* (New York, NY: James Pott & co, 1887), pp. 6, 8, 9, accessed August 5, 2014, books.google.com/books?id=sbs-AAAAYAAJ.

9. Fanny J. Crosby, "Blessed Assurance," in *Hymns of Truth and Praise* (Fort Dodge, IA: Gospel Perpetuating Publishers, 1971), hymn 394.

The Discipline of Prayer

1. R. A. Torrey, quoted in Edythe Draper, *Drapers's book of Quotations for the Christian World* (Wheaton, IL: Tyndale House Publishers, 1992), quotation 9017.

2. Andrew Murray, *Lord, Teach us to Pray* (Philadelphia, PA: Henry Altemus, 1896), 11.

3. Ibid., 2.

4. Ibid., 3.

5. Anonymous, in Brian Gunning, *The Church at Work*, 93.

6. Murray, *Lord, Teach Us to Pray*, 1.

7. Ibid., 7.

8. Ibid., 8.

9. Ibid., 19.

10. Helen H. Lemmel, "Turn Your Eyes Upon Jesus," in *Hymns of Truth and Praise*, hymn 495.

11. Elliot, *Keep a Quiet Heart*, 111.

12. Murray, *Lord, Teach Us to Pray*, 12-13.

13. Amy Carmichael, quoted in Elliot, *Keep a Quiet Heart*, 113-115.

14. Leonard Ravenhill, *Why Revival Tarries* (Bloomington, MN: Bethany House Publishers, 1959), 25.

15. Mike Attwood, *"Christ our Forerunner – Prayer"* (Presentation, Workers and Elders Conference: Overland Park, KS, October 10, 2012), Mp3, 00:21:12, accessed October 9, 2014, http://www.shawneebiblechapel.org/messages/mp3/WEC/2012-WEC-06-Atwood-Mike-Christ-Our-Forerunner-Prayer.mp3.

16. Central Intelligence Agency, "The World," *The World Factbook*, accessed August 5, 2014, https://www.cia.gov/library/publications/the-world-factbook/geos/xx.html.

The Discipline of Prayer (cont.)

17. John Newton, quoted in Draper, *Draper's Book of Quotations*, quotation 9000.
18. Brian Gunning, *The Church at Work*, 31-32.
19. Martin Luther, quoted in Draper, *Draper's Book of Quotations*, quotation 8816.

The Discipline of Purity

1. Strong, *Strong's with Tense Voice and Mood*, G5485 charis - G5486 charisma.
2. Carolyn McCulley, *Did I Kiss Marriage Goodbye?*, 32.
3. John Calvin, quoted in Carolyn McCulley, *Did I Kiss Marriage Goodbye?*, p.33.
4. John Piper, *Desiring God: Meditations of a Christian Hedonist* (Sisters, OR: Multnomah, 1996), 250.
5. Edith Stein, quoted in Mary Hestor Valentine, *Saints for Modern Women* (Chicago, IL: T. More Press, 1987), 163.
6. I would like to acknowledge my debt for many of the thoughts in this section, including the illustration of Odysseus and Jason, to a presentation by Lawrence Koo, *"Gay and Following Jesus"* (Nav20's National Conference: Colorado Springs, CO: Sep. 6, 2014).
7. Jennifer R. March, *Dictionary of Classical Mythology, 2ⁿᵈ Ed.* (Oxford: Oxbow Books, 2014), 445-446.
8. Jim Elliot, quoted in Elisabeth Elliot, *Shadow of the Almighty: The Life and Testament of Jim Elliot* (New York, NY: Harper, 1958), 152.
9. "Matthew Henry Quotes," *goodreads,* accessed June 20, 2014, http://www.goodreads.com/author/quotes/91281.Matthew_Henry.
10. F. B. Meyer, "Key Words #14: Our Walk," *Ephesians: A Daily Devotional Commentary*, accessed August 5, 2014, http://www.gotothebible.com/HTML/Sermons/EphesiansCommentaryMeyer ch14.html.
11. Thayer, *Thayer's Greek Definitions*, G2513 katharos.
12. Bethany Juedes, *"A Single Woman's Reflections on Living for the Lord among Single Godly Men"* (personal communication with the author, 2010).
13. Leslie Ludy, "There's This Guy: Responding to the distraction of attraction," *Set Apart Girl* March/April 2013, pp. 43-44. Accessed May 4, 2013, http://setapartgirl.com/magazine/issue/2013/mar-apr.
14. Bethany Juedes, *A Single Woman's Reflections.*
15. Jane Porter, *The Scottish Chiefs. Vol.1* (Andrus and Judd, 1835), 65.
16. F.B. Meyer, "Chapter 18: Receiving and Reigning," *Joshua*, accessed August 5, 2014, books.google.com/books?isbn=1619581175.
17. Bethany Juedes, *A Single Woman's Reflections.*
18. Charles H. Spurgeon, "Mahanaim, or Hosts of Angels," in *The Metropolitan Tabernacle Pulpit: Sermons Preached and Revised by C. H. Spurgeon during the year 1880, Vol. XXVI* (London: Passmore & Alabaster, 1881), 371.

Conclusion

1. Leonard Ravenhill, quoted in David Bercot, "Leonard Ravenhill," *Scroll Publishing*, accessed August 5, 2014, http://www.scrollpublishing.com/store/Ravenhill.html.
2. Keith Green, "Asleep in the Light," *Keith Green: The Greatest Hits* (Sparrow Records, 2008), Mp3.
3. John Calvin, *Institutes of the Christian Religion, Vol. 1*, ed. John T. McNeil (Louisville, KY: Westminster John Knott Press, 1960), 108, accessed August 5, 2014, books.google.com/books?isbn=1611640946.
4. C. S. Lewis, *The Collected Letters of C. S. Lewis, Vol. III*, ed. Walter Hooper (New York, NY: HarperCollins Publishers, 2007), 247, accessed August 5, 2014, books.google.com/books?isbn=0060819227.
5. William Cowper, quoted in Draper, *Draper's Book of Quotations*, quotation 6074.

Disciplines of the Heart:
Study Guide

Lesson #1: Does God Have Your Heart?

1. Consider why your heart ought to belong to God:
   a. Rom. 11:36; Acts 17:28

   b. Col. 1:16; Ps. 24:1-2

   c. 1 Cor. 6:10; 1 Pet. 1:19

2. Define the word "redeem."

3. How does a person become more godly in character and behavior (2 Cor. 3:18; Dan. 11:32b)?

4. Look up 1 Corinthians 6:20. Consider the way you are living; does your life reflect that your heart belongs to God?

Suggested memory verse:
"For you were bought at a price; therefore glorify God in your body and in your spirit, which are God's" (1 Cor. 6:20).

Lesson #2: Falling in Love With the Lord

1. What are some things you love about the Lord?

2. In your own words, explain what it means to *"pray without ceasing"* (1 Thess. 5:17).

3. How are we to pray?
   a. Luke 11:5-10, 18:1-8

   b. John 15:7

   c. Jas. 5:16-18

   d. Matt. 21:21-22; 1 Tim. 2:8; Jas. 1:5

   e. Col. 4:2; Phil. 4:6

   f. Eph. 6:18; 1 Thess. 5:17

4. For each of the general activities listed below, indicate specific, practical ways you plan to foster your relationship with God:

   a. Listening to the Lord

   b. Talking with the Lord

   c. Talking about the Lord

   d. Spending time with the Lord

Suggested memory verse:
"And you shall love the Lord your God with all your heart, and with all your soul, and with all your might" (Deut. 6:5).

Lesson #3: What Is the Heart?

1. Use the Scripture references to fill in the blanks, describing the three components of a person.

Spirit	Soul	
		1 Thess. 5:23
Eccl. 12:7	*Matt. 10:28; Rev. 6:9*	Not eternal
Job 32:8; Prov. 20:27	Self-conscious	Earth-conscious
Heavenly	*Gen. 2:7; Acts 2:43*	Animal

2. What types of things pertain to the activities of the heart?
   a. Prov. 14:10; John 16:22; Rom. 9:2-3

   b. Jer. 17:9; Matt. 15:19

   c. Acts 11:23; 2 Cor. 9:7; Heb. 4:12

   d. Mark 2:6; Luke 1:51; Heb. 4:12

3. What is the natural state of the human heart (Jer. 17:9)? What is God's answer to this (Jer. 24:7, 29:13)?

Suggested memory verse:
"Now may the God of peace Himself sanctify you completely; and may your whole spirit, soul, and body be preserved blameless at the coming of our Lord Jesus Christ" (1 Thess. 5:23).

Lesson #4: A Heart After God's Own Heart

1. What does God know about your heart (Ps. 44:21; Luke 9:47; Heb. 4:12)?

2. What type of heart does God appreciate and how is it cultivated (Acts 13:22)?

3. Look up the following verses and write down some practical considerations when seeking the specific will of God for your life. Remember that you first need to be living in accordance with the general will of God as revealed in Scripture!
    a. Prov. 16:1, 9

    b. Prov. 11:14

    c. Col. 3:15

    d. Ps. 37:4

4. What was the nation of Israel rebuked for in Matthew 15:8 and Mark 7:6? Is it possible for Christians today to err in the same way?

5. Consider the following:
   a. Is my heart broken and contrite?

   b. How close is my heart to God?

   c. What is the desire of my heart?

   d. Is my heart like the Lord's heart?

   e. Am I obeying all that God's Word has revealed to me?

Suggested memory verse:
"I have found David, the son of Jesse, a man after My own heart, who will do all My will" (Acts 13:22b).

Lesson #5: The Penitent Heart

1. Explain, in your own words, the word "penitent."

2. How do we know that merely believing in God does not ensure a right relationship with Him (Jas. 2:19)?

3. Does Scripture tell us to ask for forgiveness for our sins or to confess/acknowledge our sins (Lev. 26:40; Ps. 32:5; 1 Jn. 1:9)? What is the associated promise given to Christians in the last verse?

4. Take time to look over your life and contemplate what unconfessed sins need to be addressed:
   a. Sins of commission (wrong things I do)

   b. Sins of omission (right things I do not do)

   c. *"Secret sins"* (Ps. 90:8)

   d. *"Presumptuous sins"* (Ps. 19:13)

5. When I repent of my sin, what am I telling God I desire to do (2 Cor. 7:10)?

Suggested memory verse:
"If we confess our sins, He is faithful and just to forgive us our sins and to cleanse us from all unrighteousness" (1 Jn. 1:9).

Lesson #6: The Pure Heart

1. In your own words, describe what "pure" means.

2. *Katharos*, one of the Greek words translated as "pure" in the New Testament, is also used to speak of how precious metals are refined by fire and of how a vine is pruned in order to produce more fruit. Explain the connection between these ideas and how moral purity is cultivated in a life.

3. Does purity involve only actions or does it apply to what we think about as well (Prov. 23:7, 24:9; Romans 1:32)?

4. The Lord works to purify His people, but we certainly do not want to resist that work in us. What are some practical things you will do to foster purity in your life?

5. God blesses those who have pure hearts (Ps. 73:1); what is the greatest benefit of purity (Ps. 24:3-6; Matt. 5:8)?

Suggested memory verse:
"Draw near to God and He will draw near to you. Cleanse your hands, you sinners; and purify your hearts, you double-minded" (Jas. 4:8).

Lesson #7: The Perfect Heart

1. What does it mean to have a "perfect" heart?

2. If your heart is *complete*, it will be *ready* for the work that is intended. What are God's expectations for your life (Gal. 5:22-26; Eph. 2:10)?

3. How is a perfect (some Bible versions will say "loyal," "single," or "whole") heart expressed in daily life?
    a. 1 Chron. 12:38

    b. 1 Chron. 28:9

    c. 1 Chron. 29:9

    d. 2 Chron. 19:9

    e. Eph. 6:5

    f. Col. 3:22

4. Consider: what are the consequences of living a Christian life without having a perfect heart?

5. How can those who seek to have a perfect heart before God be encouraged (2 Chron. 16:9)?

Suggested memory verse:
"Teach me Your way, O LORD; I will walk in Your truth; **unite my heart** *to fear Your name"* (Ps. 86:11, emphasis added).

Lesson #8: The Prepared Heart

1. A prepared heart is the determination of the inner person prior to a new or renewed seeking after the Lord. What attitudes are associated with this resolve?

   a. 1 Sam. 7:3

   b. Ezra 7:10

   c. Ps. 10:17

2. Investigate what Scripture has to say about Ezra, and comment on how having a prepared heart influenced his life (e.g. Ezra 7:6, 10, 25; 8:21-23; 9:3-6; 10:1).

3. What is a believer's responsibility in preparing his or her heart for the Lord (1 Chron. 29:18; 2 Chron. 19:3, 12:14; Job 11:13; Ps. 10:17)? Explain your answer.

4. What is an idol? Take some time to reflect on whether there are any idols in your heart/life.

Suggested memory verse:
"For Ezra had prepared his heart to seek the Law of the LORD, and to do it, and to teach statutes and ordinances in Israel" (Ezra 7:10).

Lesson #9: The Purposed Heart

1. In your own words, explain the phrase *"purpose of heart"* (Acts 11:23).

2. How does the story of Ruth encourage you?

3. King David wrote a personal "Psalm of Resolution" (Ps. 101). Read this psalm and write down at least one of these intentions that you will personally aspire to, along with practical ways of doing so. (Consider writing your own "Psalm of Resolution"!)

4. What does the story of Daniel and his three friends teach you about taking a stand for holiness (Dan. 1)? (Remember this was a largely unpopular move, and a resolution many would say was not in keeping with the "smallness" of the matter at hand.)

5. Identify the resolutions in the following passages:
   a. Ps. 17:3

   b. Ps. 108:1

   c. Dan. 10:12

   d. 2 Cor. 9:7

   e. Acts 11:23

   f. 2 Thess. 3:5

Suggested memory verse:
"When he came and had seen the grace of God, he was glad, and encouraged them all that with purpose of heart they should continue with the Lord" (Acts 11:23).

Lesson #10: The Protected Heart

1. Why is it important to guard one's heart (Matt. 12:34-35, 15:18-19)?

2. Explain how hearts are guarded according to Philippians 4:6-7.

3. On what sorts of things are we to allow our minds to dwell (Phil. 4:8)?

4. How will you defend your heart from discontentment? Consider Psalm 84:11, Romans 8:28, Philippians 4:19, and 1 Thessalonians 5:18.

5. Is there something that has gained ground in your heart or mind that shouldn't be there? What practical steps will you take to guard your heart?

Suggested memory verses:
"Be anxious for nothing, but in everything by prayer and supplication, with thanksgiving, let your requests be made known to God; and the peace of God, which surpasses all understanding, will guard your hearts and minds through Christ Jesus. Finally, brethren, whatever things are true, whatever things are noble, whatever things are just, whatever things are pure, whatever things are lovely, whatever things are of good report, if there is any virtue and if there is anything praiseworthy—meditate on these things" (Phil. 4:6-8).

Lesson #11: Personal Discipline

1. Take time and reflect on whether your life is controlled by anything other than God (these could be sins or things that are not inherently sinful).

2. In your own words, explain what personal discipline means.

3. What can we learn about discipline from 1 Corinthians 9:24-27? Also consider Galatians 5:16-26.

4. The Bible gives various instructions that will assist us in the work of personal discipline; identify and explain those found in the following verses: Titus 2:11-14; 1 Peter 1:13, 4:7, 5:8. Can you think of other such instructions?

5. Any Christian who is serious about personal discipline must commit to reading, studying, and applying Scripture. Identify and explain the similitudes given for the Bible in the following verses:
   a. Ps. 119:103; Ezek. 3:1-4; Jer. 15:16

   b. Ps. 119:105

   c. Ps. 119:162

   d. Jer. 23:29

   e. 1 Pet. 2:2

Suggested memory verses:
"You therefore must endure hardship as a good soldier of Jesus Christ. No one engaged in warfare entangles himself with the affairs of this life, that he may please Him who enlisted him as a soldier" (2 Tim. 2:3-4).

Lesson #12: The Discipline of Self-Control

1. How is self-control developed in a life (Gal. 5:22-23; Eph. 5:18; 2 Pet. 1:3-4)?

2. Romans 13:13 describes various sins that result from a lack of self-control; read verse 14, then identify and explain the two-part strategy we can use to confront these:
a. Rom. 13:14a

b. Rom. 13:14b

3. For each set of verses, identify the area of life that is in focus (e.g. thoughts). Within each general area, identify something specific in your own life that needs attention, along with practical steps you plan to take to address this matter.

	Area	Needs Attention	Practical Steps
Prov. 23:7a; Rom. 12:2; 1 Pet. 1:13a			
Prov. 16:32; John 14:1; Phil. 4:6			
Ps. 19:14; Prov. 16:32, 29:11; Matt. 12:36; Eph. 4:29			
2 Cor. 9:6-8; 1 Tim. 4:7-8, 5:6; 2 Tim. 2:4			

Suggested memory verses:
"And everyone who competes for the prize is temperate in all things. Now they do it to obtain a perishable crown, but we for an imperishable crown. Therefore I run thus: not with uncertainty. Thus I fight: not as one who beats the air. But I discipline my body and bring it into subjection, lest, when I have preached to others, I myself should become disqualified" (1 Cor. 9:25-27).

Lesson #13: The Discipline of Contentment

1. With what are we to be content (1 Tim. 6:8; Luke 3:14b; Heb. 13:5)? Are there any reasons we should not be content (Josh. 7:7; Phil. 3:12-14)?

2. With what does God equate covetousness in Colossians 3:5? Why do you think this is?

3. The Kingdom of Judah was rebuked for covetousness in Jeremiah 6:13. Examine the context of this verse by looking at the surrounding Scripture. What behaviors were associated with the covetousness of the Jews, and what were the consequences?

4. Explain one strategy for combating each of the three following manifestations of discontentment:

   a. Covetousness

   b. Self-pity

   c. Depression

Suggested memory verses:
"Not that I speak in regard to need, for I have learned in whatever state I am, to be content: I know how to be abased, and I know how to abound. Everywhere and in all things I have learned both to be full and to be hungry, both to abound and to suffer need. I can do all things through Christ who strengthens me" (Phil. 4:11-13).

Lesson #14: The Discipline of Thankfulness

1. Under what circumstances are we to give thanks to God (Eph. 5:20; Col. 3:15, 17; 1 Thess. 5:18; 1 Tim. 2:1)?

2. How is it possible to give thanks when it is the last thing you feel like doing?

3. Identify reasons to praise and give thanks to God.
   a. Ps. 33:1, 92:1

   b. 2 Sam. 22:4; Rev. 4:11, 5:12

   c. 1 Cor. 15:57; 2 Cor. 2:14

   d. 2 Cor. 9:15; Col. 1:12

   e. 2 Thess. 1:3

   f. 2 Pet. 1:3

4. Write down some things for which you are thankful to God.

Suggested memory verse:
"And let the peace of God rule in your hearts, to which also you were called in one body; and be thankful" (Col. 3:15).

Lesson #15: The Discipline of Faithfulness

1. There are various roles in which God is said to be faithful; identify these and explain how He demonstrates His faithfulness in each.
    a. Deut. 7:9; Mal. 3:6

    b. 1 Pet. 4:19; Heb. 1:3

    c. Heb. 2:17, 7:25

2. Read *The Parable of the Talents*, as recorded in Matthew 25:14-30.
    a. How long was the householder absent (v. 25)? What is the application?

    b. In this narrative each servant received a different amount of money. While all Christians have the same "amounts" of certain things, like time and the privilege of prayer, other gifts from God are diverse. What are some examples of the latter?

    c. Look at the amounts given the first two servants and their rewards – was the reward based on the final amount of money they presented to the householder?

    d. Who is responsible for judging the servants' faithfulness (v. 19)?

    e. What was the reward for faithfulness (v. 21, 23)?

    f. What was the underlying reason for the last servant's unfaithfulness (v. 24-25)?

180

3. Is your life marked by faithfulness? Prayerfully consider what areas of your life are in need of a greater demonstration of faithfulness.

Suggested memory verse:
"Moreover, it is required in stewards that one be found faithful" (1 Cor. 4:2).

Lesson #16: The Discipline of Joy

1. Explain what joy is, biblically speaking. Is rejoicing a reaction or an action?

2. Where does joy come from (Ps. 16:11; Jer. 2:13; Matt. 25:21, 23; John 17:13)?

3. Considering your answer from the previous question, what causes a lack of joy in the Christian's life (Ps. 51:7-8)?

4. Reflect on the examples of Habakkuk (Hab. 3:17-19) and Paul and Silas (Acts 16:16-34). How is it possible to have joy when circumstances seem to dictate otherwise?

5. How will you cultivate joy in your life?

Suggested memory verse:
"Rejoice in the Lord always. Again I will say, Rejoice!" (Phil. 4:4).

Lesson #17: The Discipline of Patience

1. Is patience to be a characteristic of certain personality types, or of all Christians (Gal. 5:22; Eph. 4:1-2)?

2. Identify some of the situations in which patience is needed (and developed!).
   a. Jas. 5:10

   b. Jas. 5:11

   c. Gen. 12:1-4, 21:5; Heb. 6:15

   d. 1 Thess. 5:14

3. Why should our lives be characterized by patience?
    a. Ex. 34:6; Phil. 1:6; Rom. 15:5

    b. 2 Cor. 6:4; 1 Tim. 6:11; 2 Tim. 2:24-26

    c. Jas. 1:2-4

    d. Luke 8:15; 2 Tim. 4:2; Rev. 2:2-3

    e. Rom. 8:25; Heb. 6:12; Jas. 5:7

4. In what ways has God demonstrated patience towards you?

Suggested memory verse:
"Wait on the Lord: be of good courage, and He shall strengthen your heart; wait, I say, on the Lord" (Ps. 27:14).

Lesson #18: The Discipline of Submission

1. What do we learn about submission from the following verses (Rom. 10:3; Heb. 12:9; Jas. 4:6-7; 1 Pet. 5:5)?

2. Christians are to submit to the will of God; what are three characteristics of His will mentioned in Romans 12:1-2?

3. Identify the order of submission in the following interpersonal relationships:
   a. Eph. 6:1-3

   b. Eph. 5:22, 24; Col. 3:18; Titus 2:5; 1 Pet. 3:1, 5

   c. Titus 2:9; 1 Pet. 2:18

   d. Rom. 13:1-5; Titus 3:1; 1 Pet. 2:13

   e. Heb. 13:17

   f. Eph. 5:21; 1 Pet. 5:5

4. Are you submitting to everything God has for you, and to the authorities He has placed in your life?

Suggested memory verses:
"Therefore He says: 'God resists the proud, but gives grace to the humble.' Therefore submit to God" (Jas. 4:6b-7a).

Lesson #19: The Discipline of Prayer

1. Read Luke 11:1-4; what applications can you make to your own prayer life?

2. Why do you think prayer is something God thinks is important for His children (Rom. 12:12; Eph. 6:18; Phil. 4:6; Col. 4:2; 1 Thess. 5:17; 1 Tim. 2:1-2)?

3. What are some reasons one's prayer life might be suffering (Ps. 66:18; Prov. 15:8, 29, 28:9; Jas. 4:2-3)?

4. How would you answer someone who says, "What is the point of prayer? Whatever God wants to happen is going to happen anyway. What is the use of *my* prayers?"

5. What is one way we can work together with fellow believers (Rom. 15:30; Eph. 6:18-19; Col. 4:3-4)?

6. This week, read some of the prayers recorded in the Bible and copy some of the requests you can use in your personal prayers. Possible examples include: Psalm 72:18-20, Nehemiah 1:5-11, Daniel 9, John 17, Ephesians 3:14-21, Colossians 1:9-14, and 1 Thessalonians 3:9-13.

Suggested memory verses:
"Continue earnestly in prayer, being vigilant in it with thanksgiving" (Col. 4:2).
"The effective, fervent prayer of a righteous man avails much" (Jas. 5:16b).

Lesson #20: The Discipline of Purity

1. All we have comes from God. What do we know about His gifts (Ps. 84:11; Jas. 1:17) and the purpose of these (Eph. 4:12-13; 1 Pet. 4:10)?

2. What is God's clear design for our sexuality?
   a. Gen. 1:27, 2:24; Mark 10:7-8, Eph. 5:31

   b. Rom. 1:24-32; 1 Cor. 6:18-19; Eph. 5:3-5; 1 Thess. 4:3

3. If you are committed to purity, consider for a moment what motivates you to this: a resolve to externally resist the enchantments of sin, or a captivation with a "better song"?

4. What do we learn from 1 Corinthians 10:12-13 concerning life's trials?

5. Does purity involve only words and actions, or might it extend to desires, motives, and thoughts (Prov. 4:23, 24:9a; Jer. 17:9; Matt. 5:28)? It may be helpful to check Thayer's definition of *katharos* (purity).

6. In your own words, explain the difference between attraction and distraction (or infatuation).

7. What are some practical steps you will take to foster the discipline of purity in your life?

Suggested memory verses:
"Therefore let him who thinks he stands take heed lest he fall. No temptation has overtaken you except such as is common to man; but God is faithful, who will not allow you to be tempted beyond what you are able, but with the temptation will also make the way of escape, that you may be able to bear it" (1 Cor. 10:12-13).
"Flee also youthful lusts; but pursue righteousness, faith, love, peace with those who call on the Lord out of a pure heart" (2 Tim. 2:22).

191

CPSIA information can be obtained
at www.ICGtesting.com
Printed in the USA
LVOW13s1519240117
522003LV00011BA/1071/P